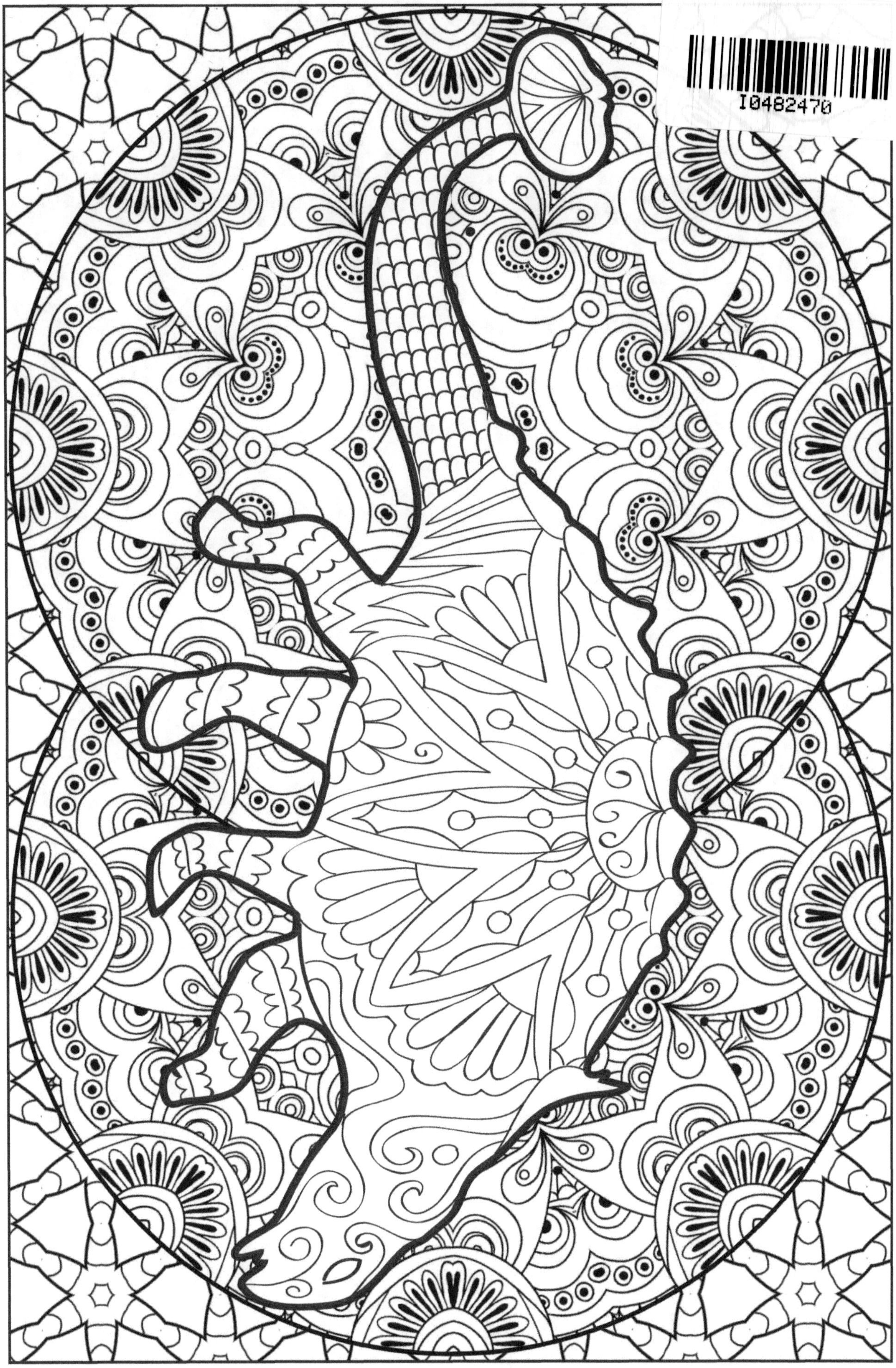

ARTISTIC DEN

DINOSAUR MANDALA
COLORING BOOK FOR ADULTS
MANDALA ADULT COLORING BOOK
VOLUME 1

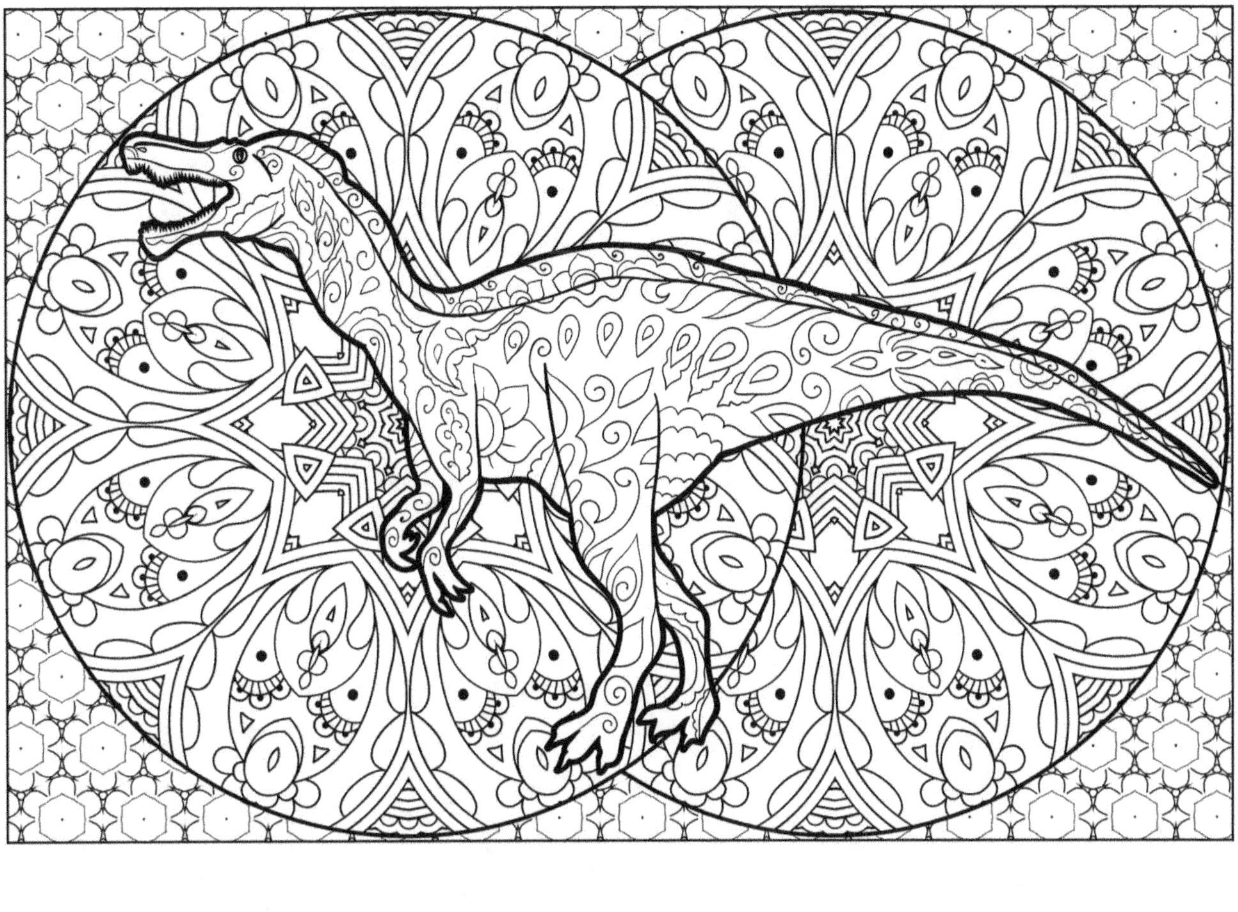

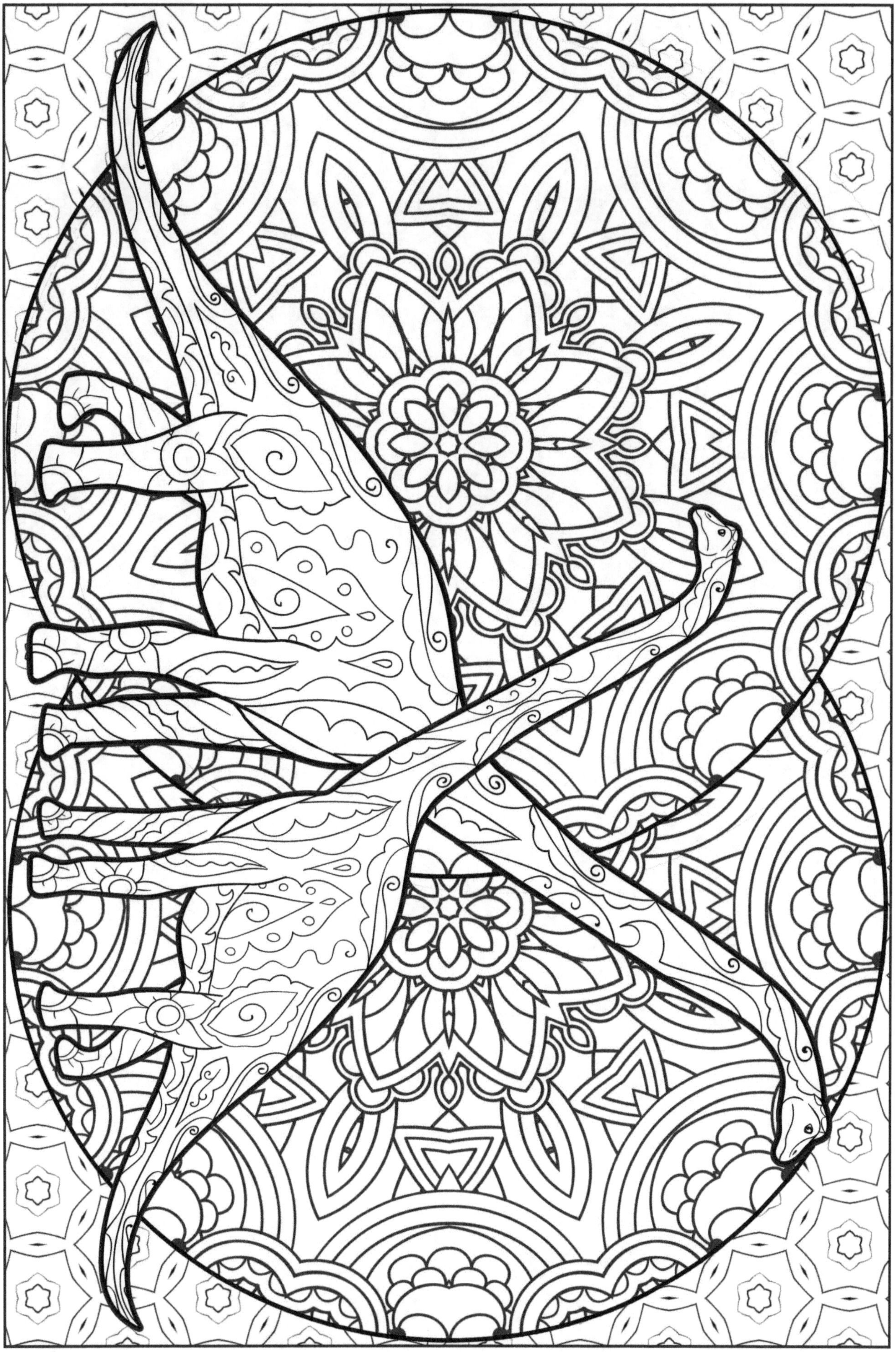

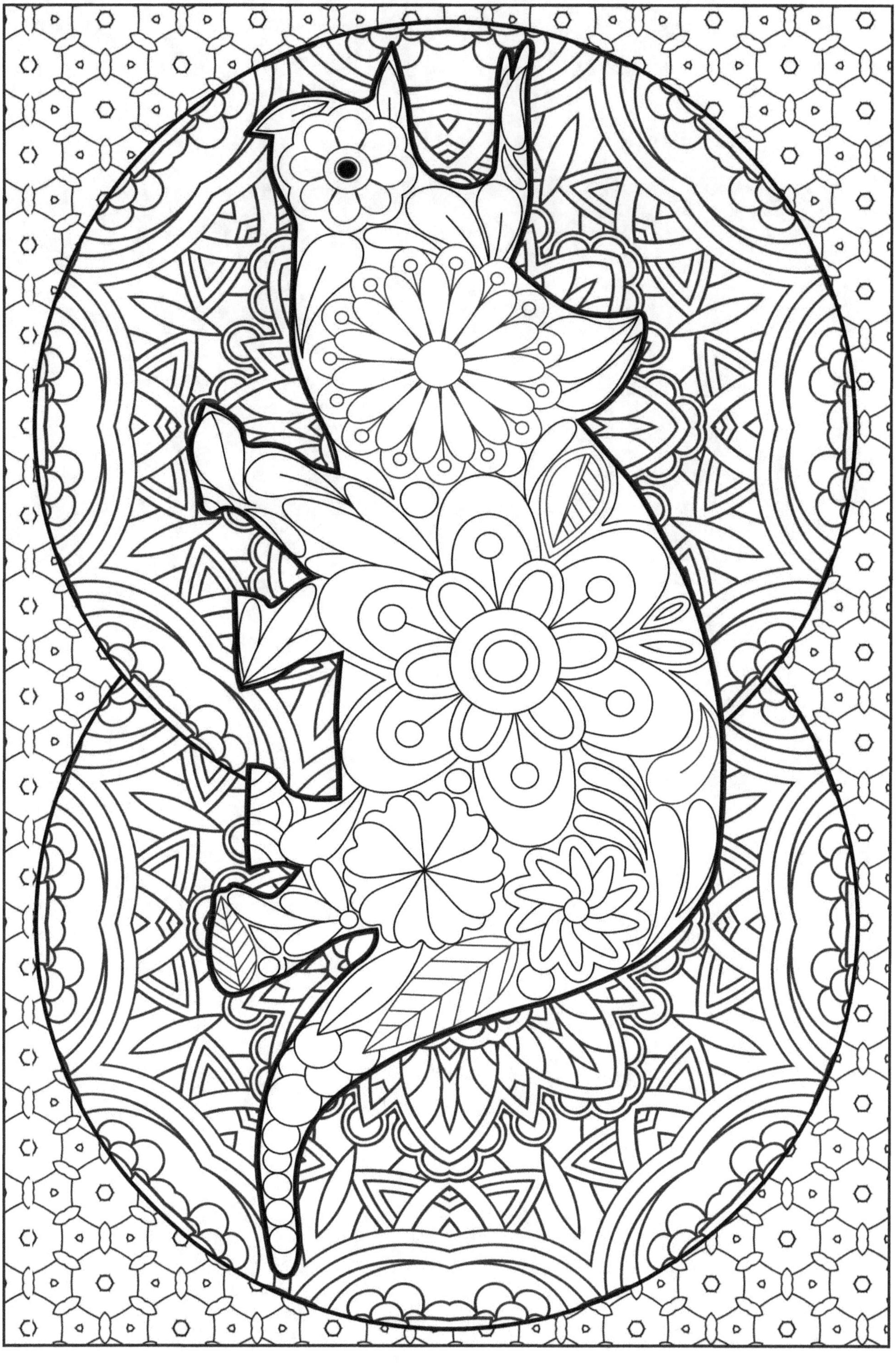

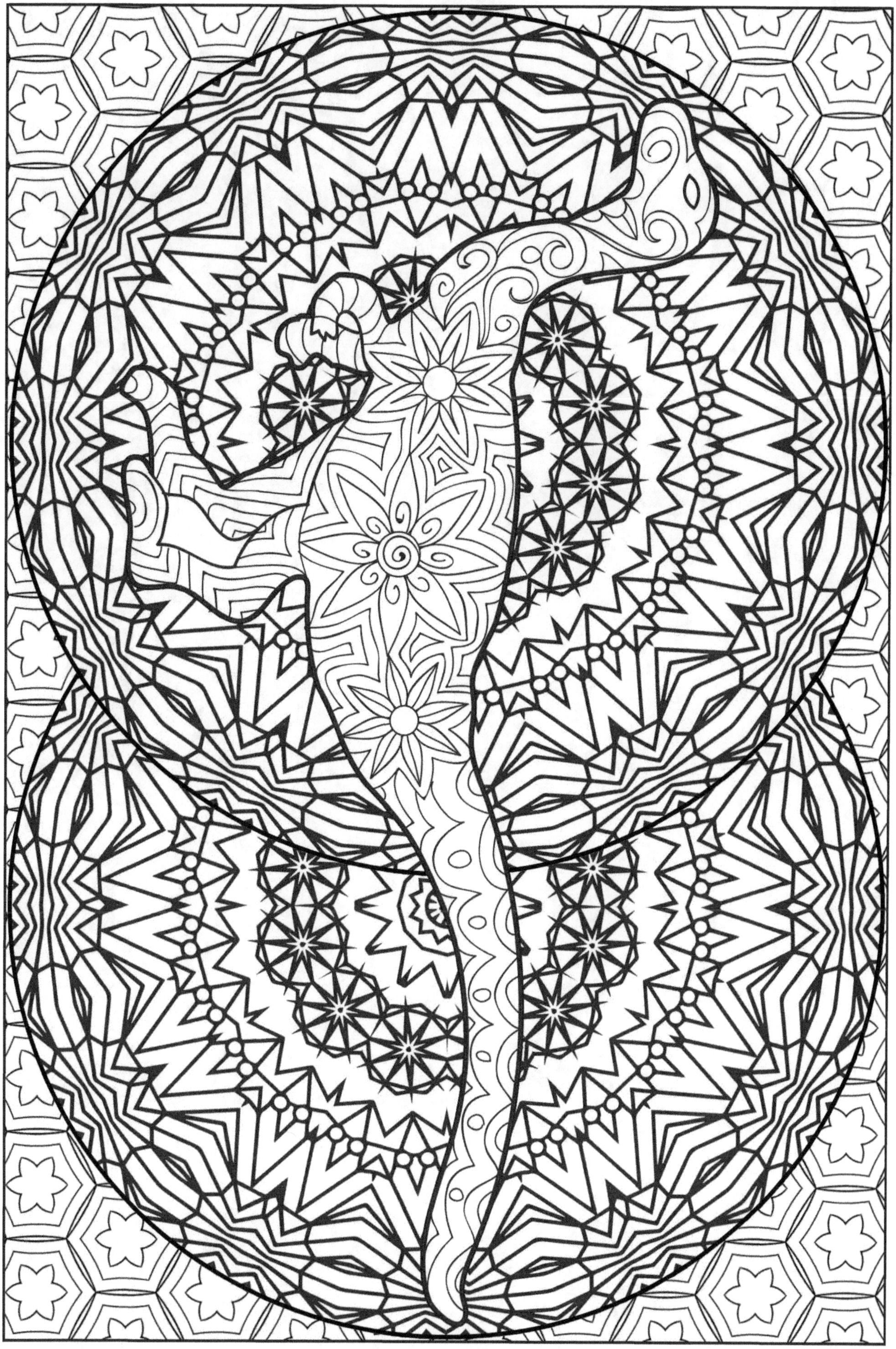

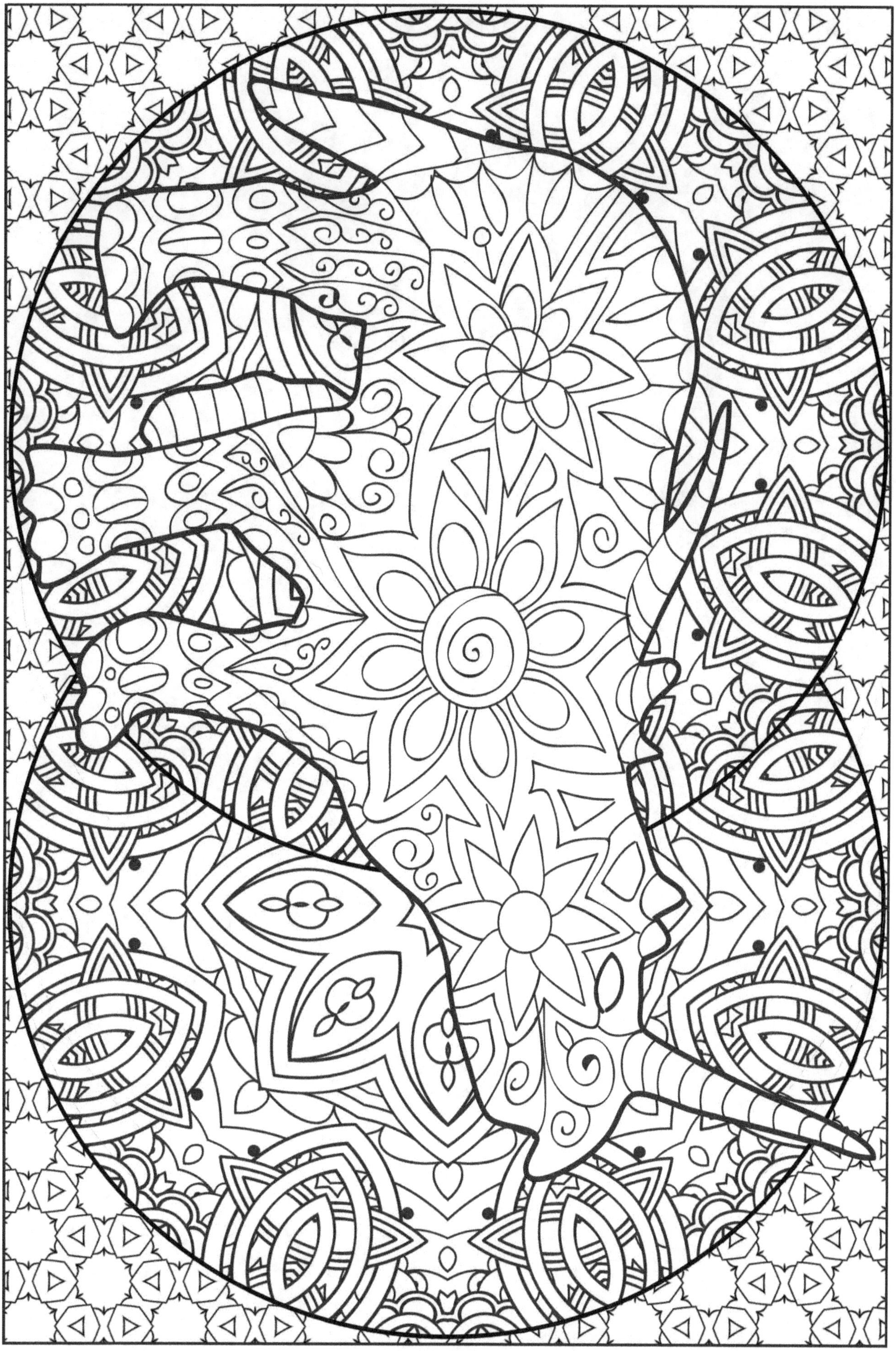

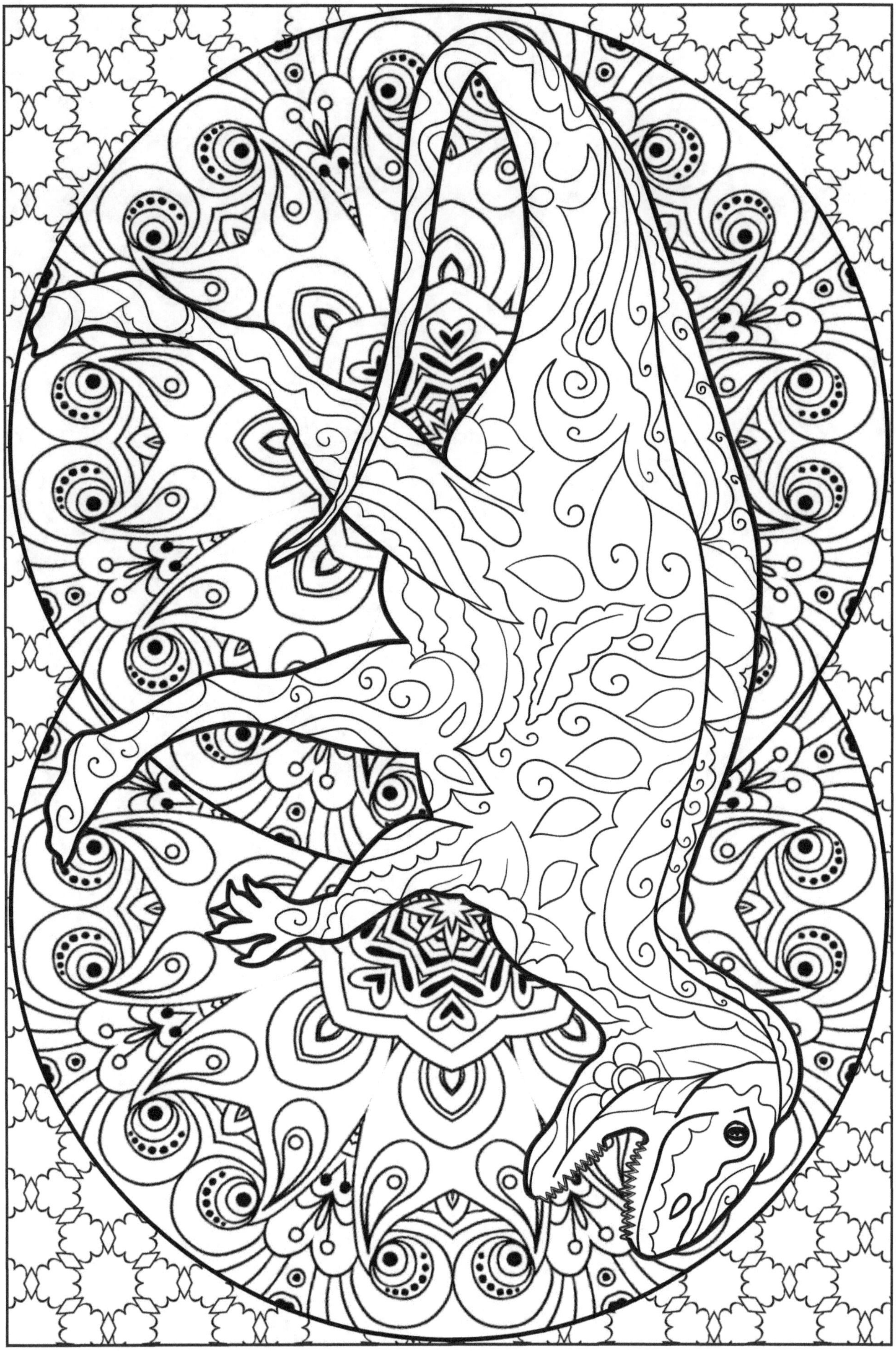

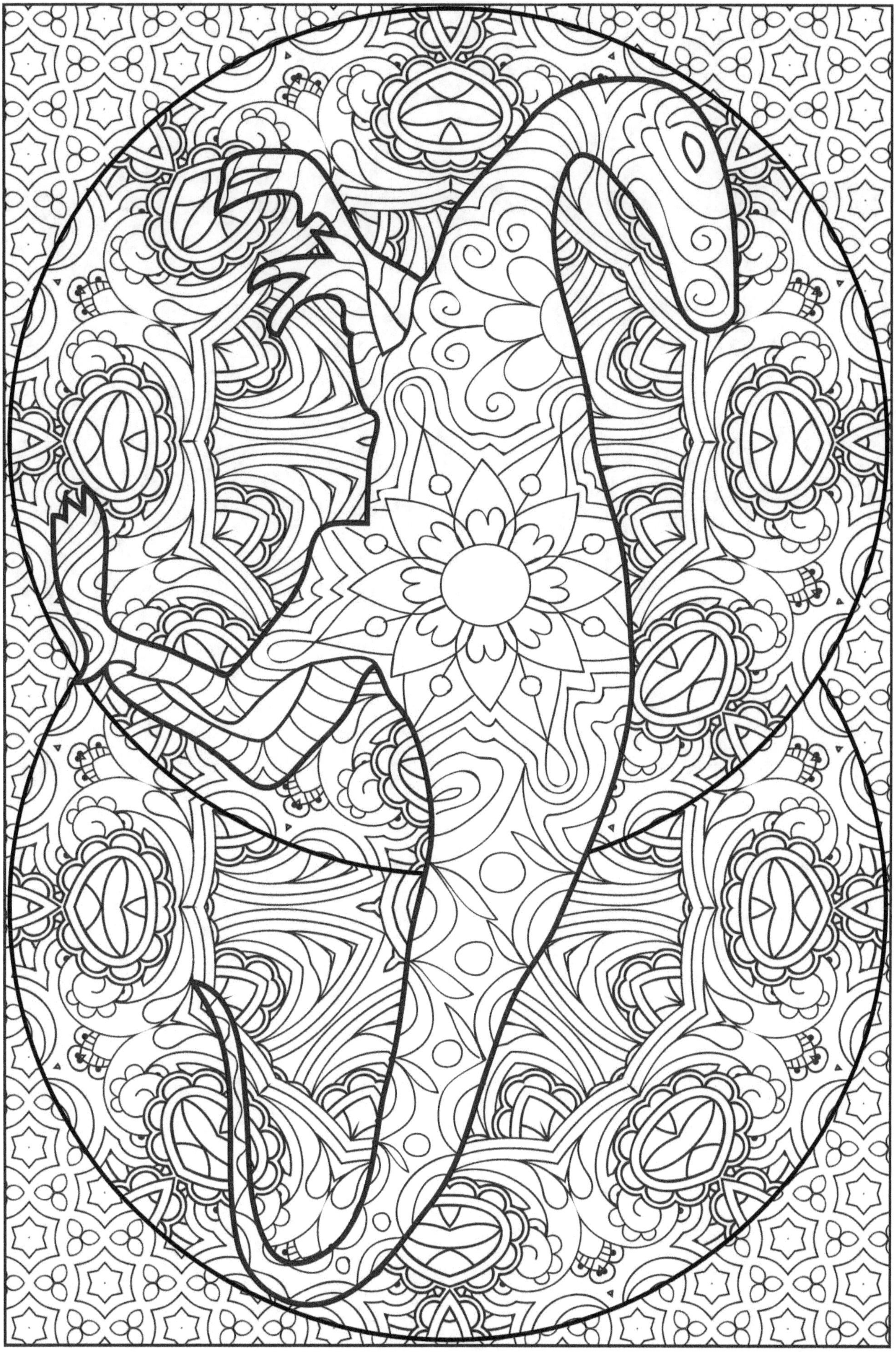

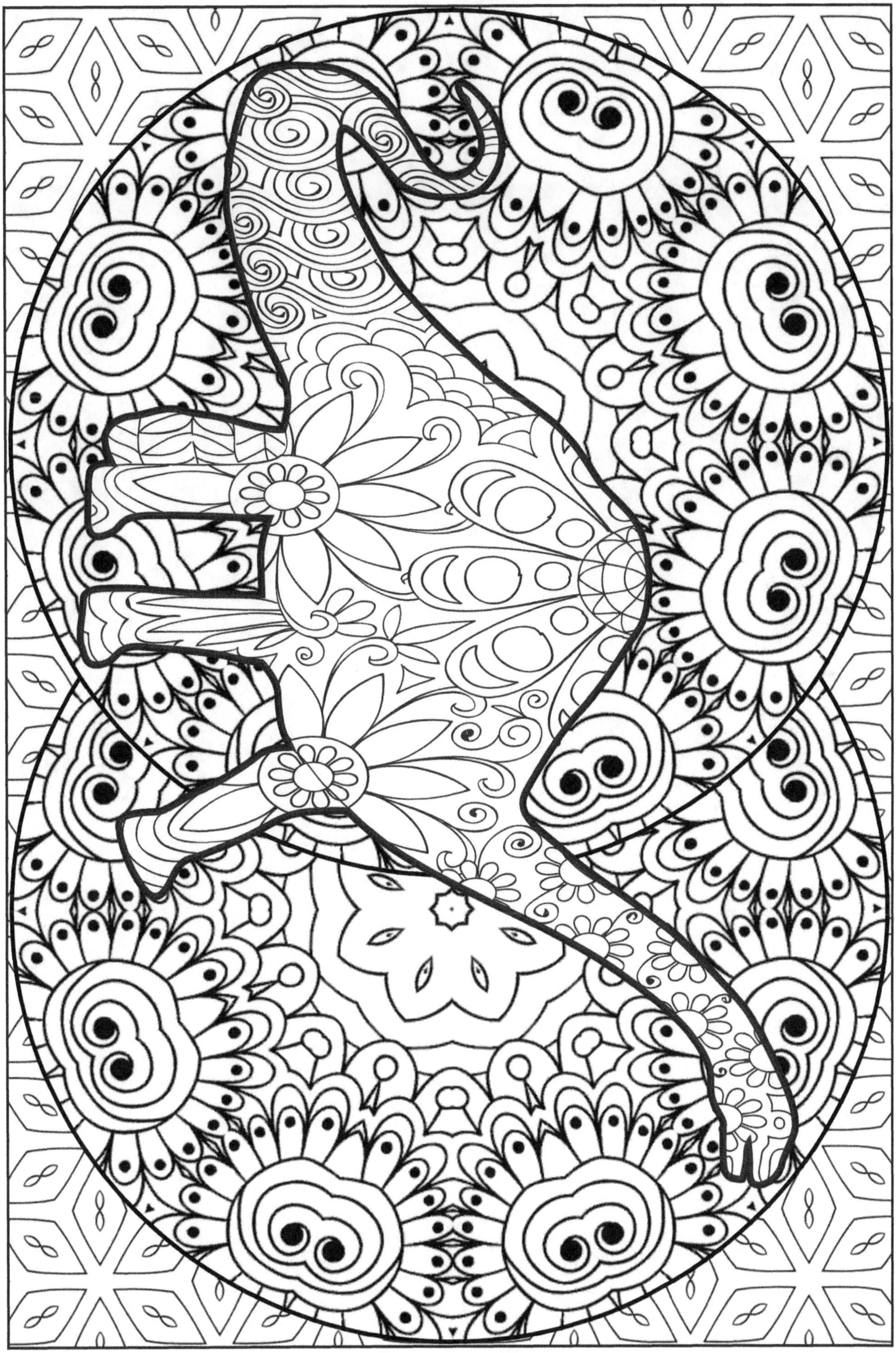

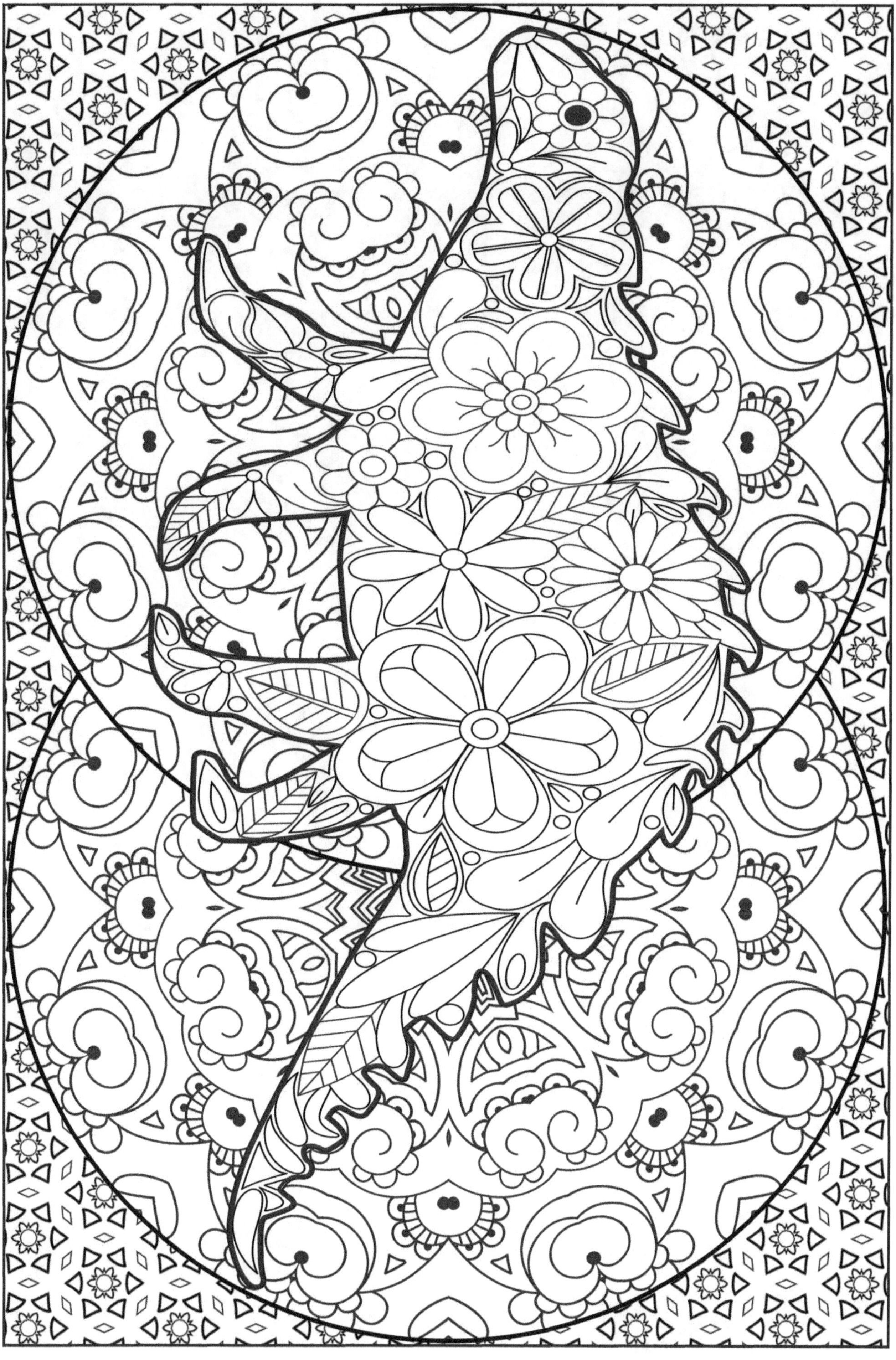

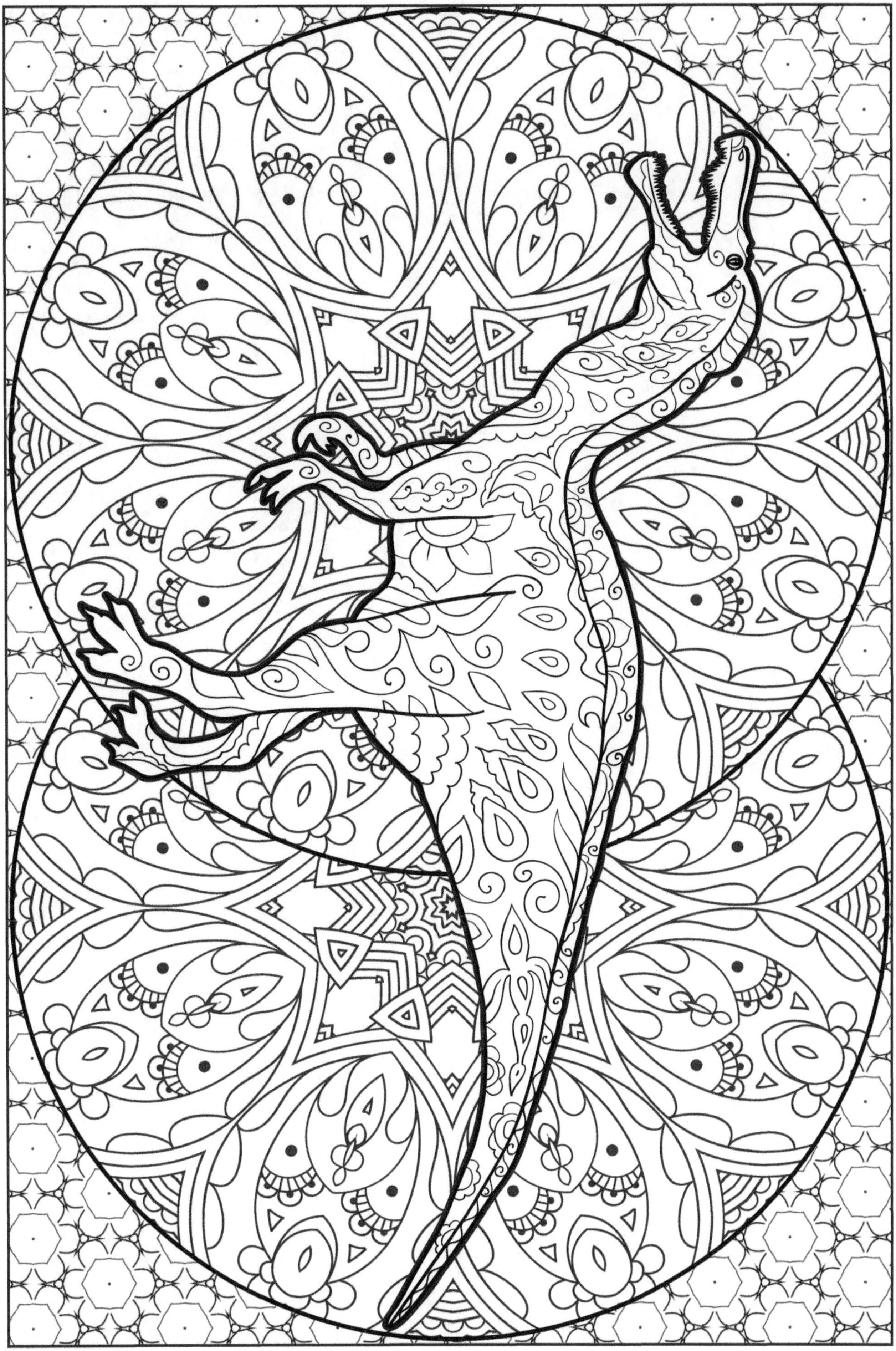

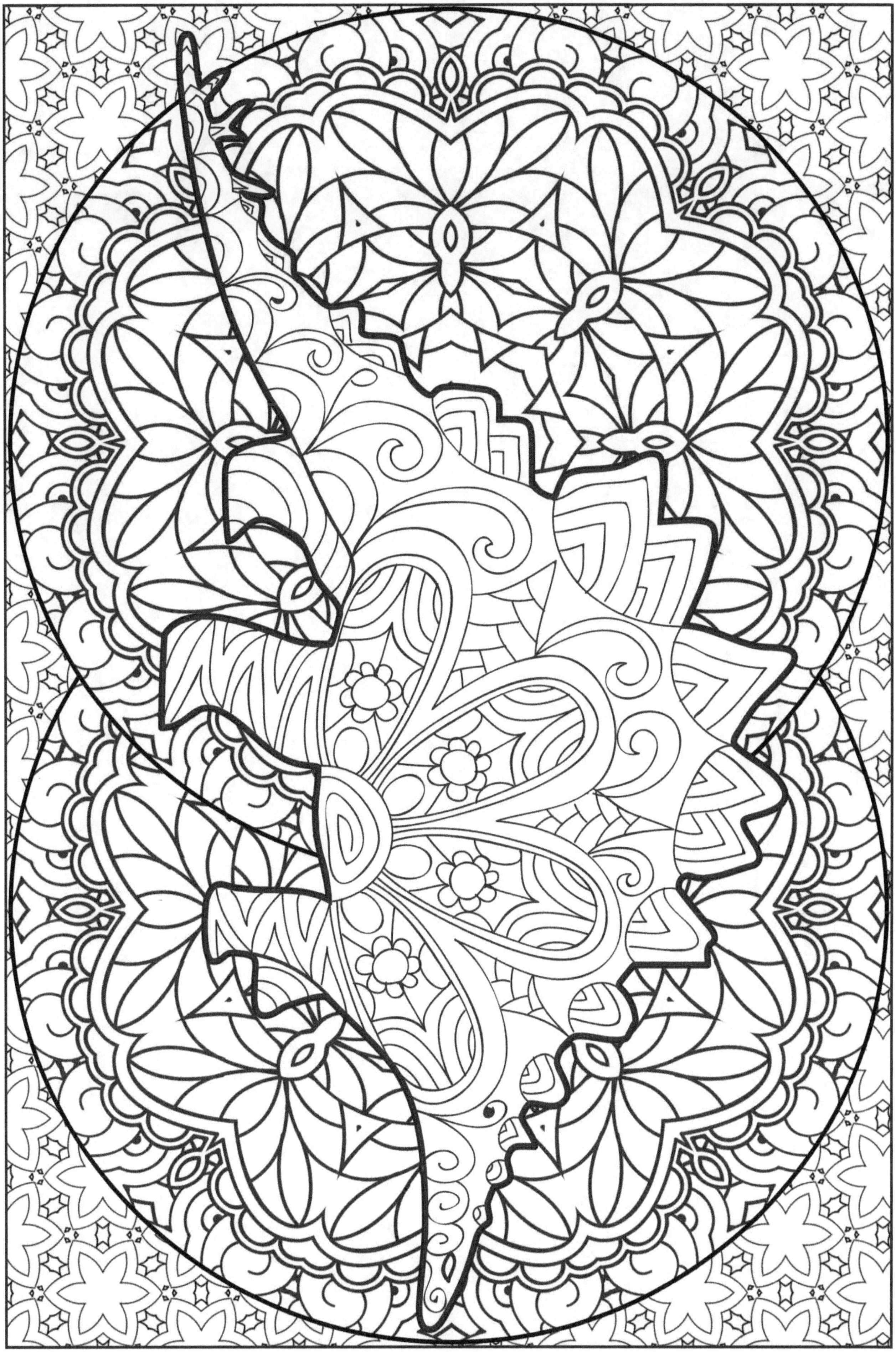

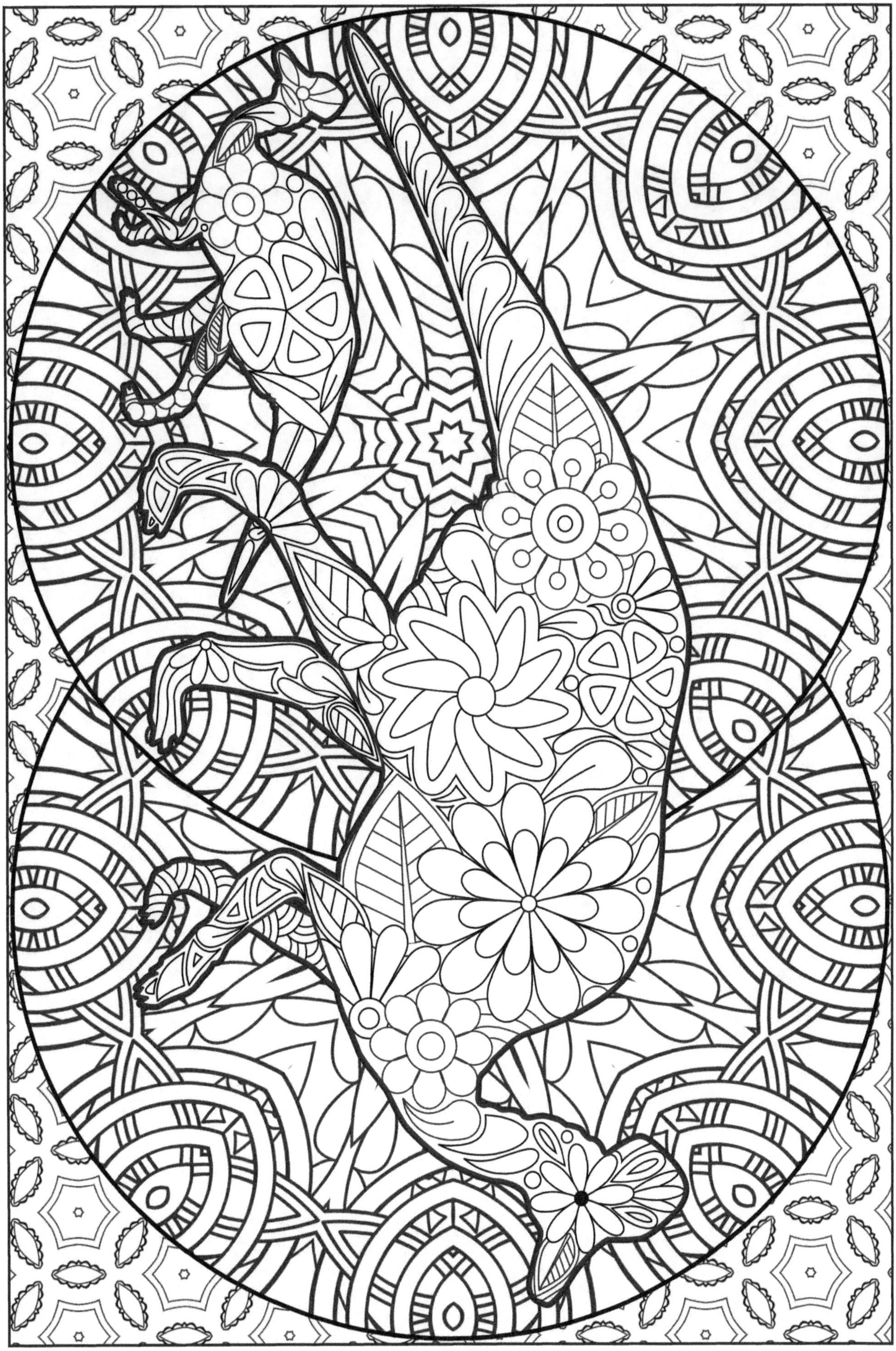

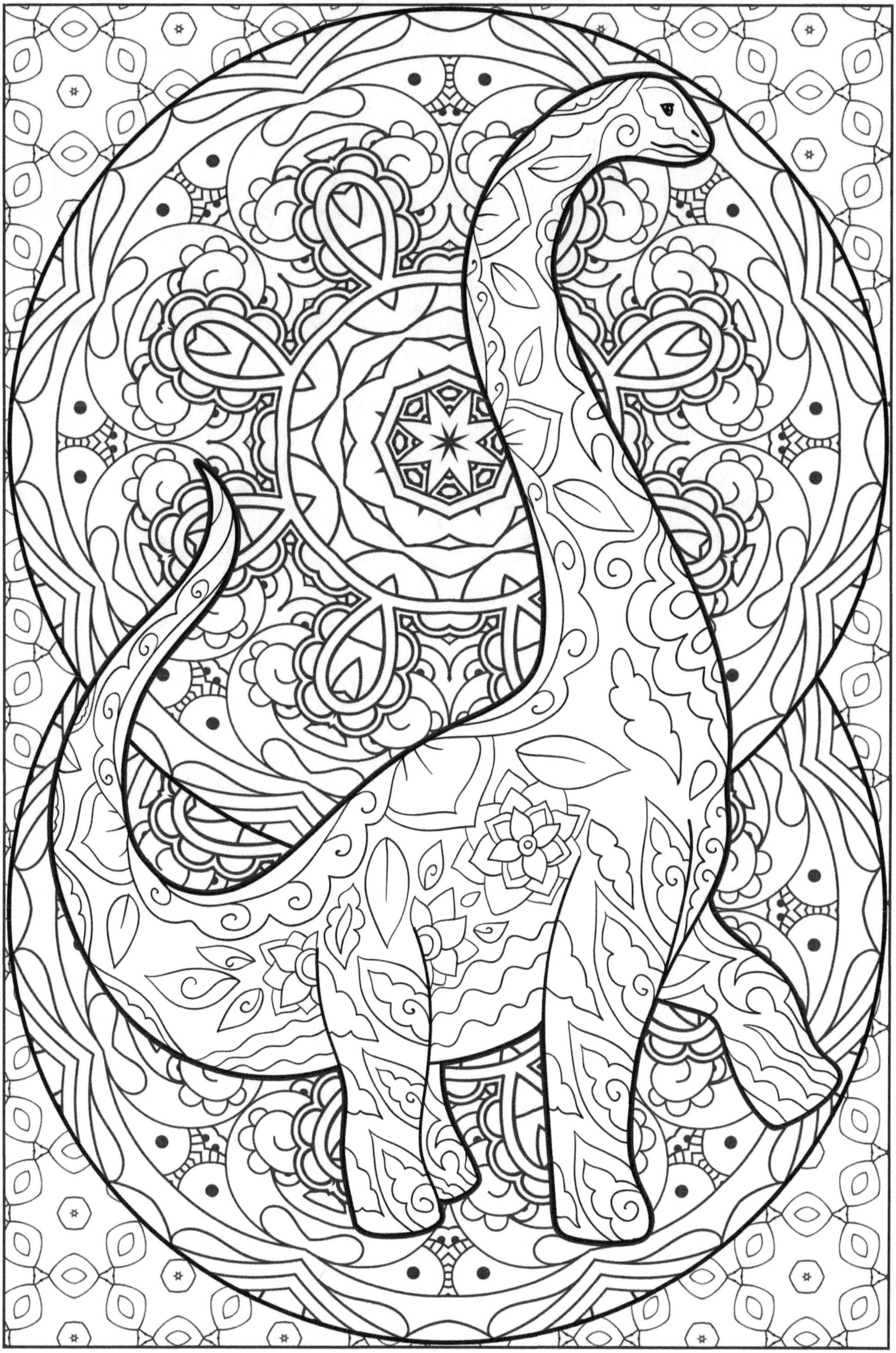

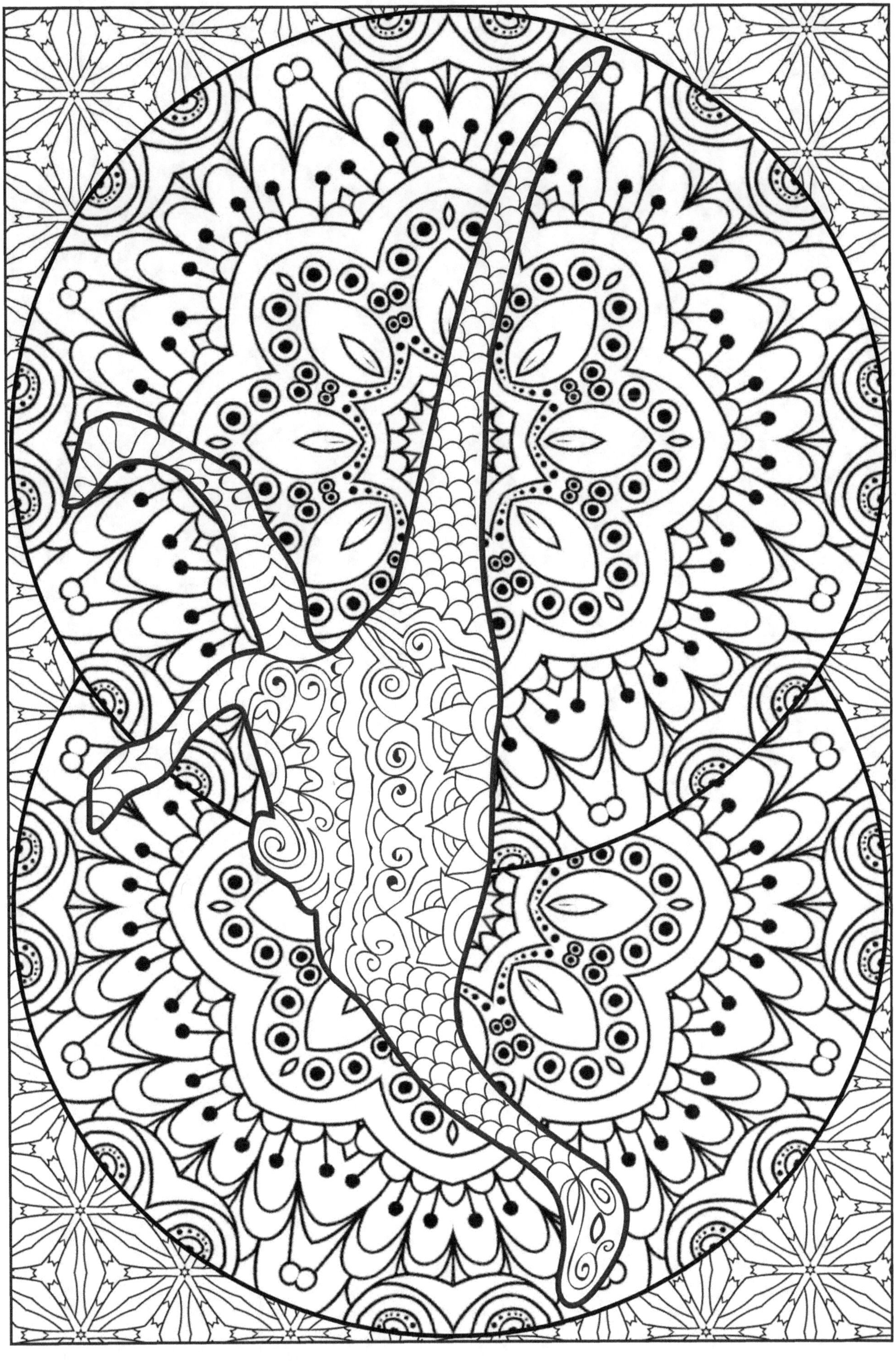

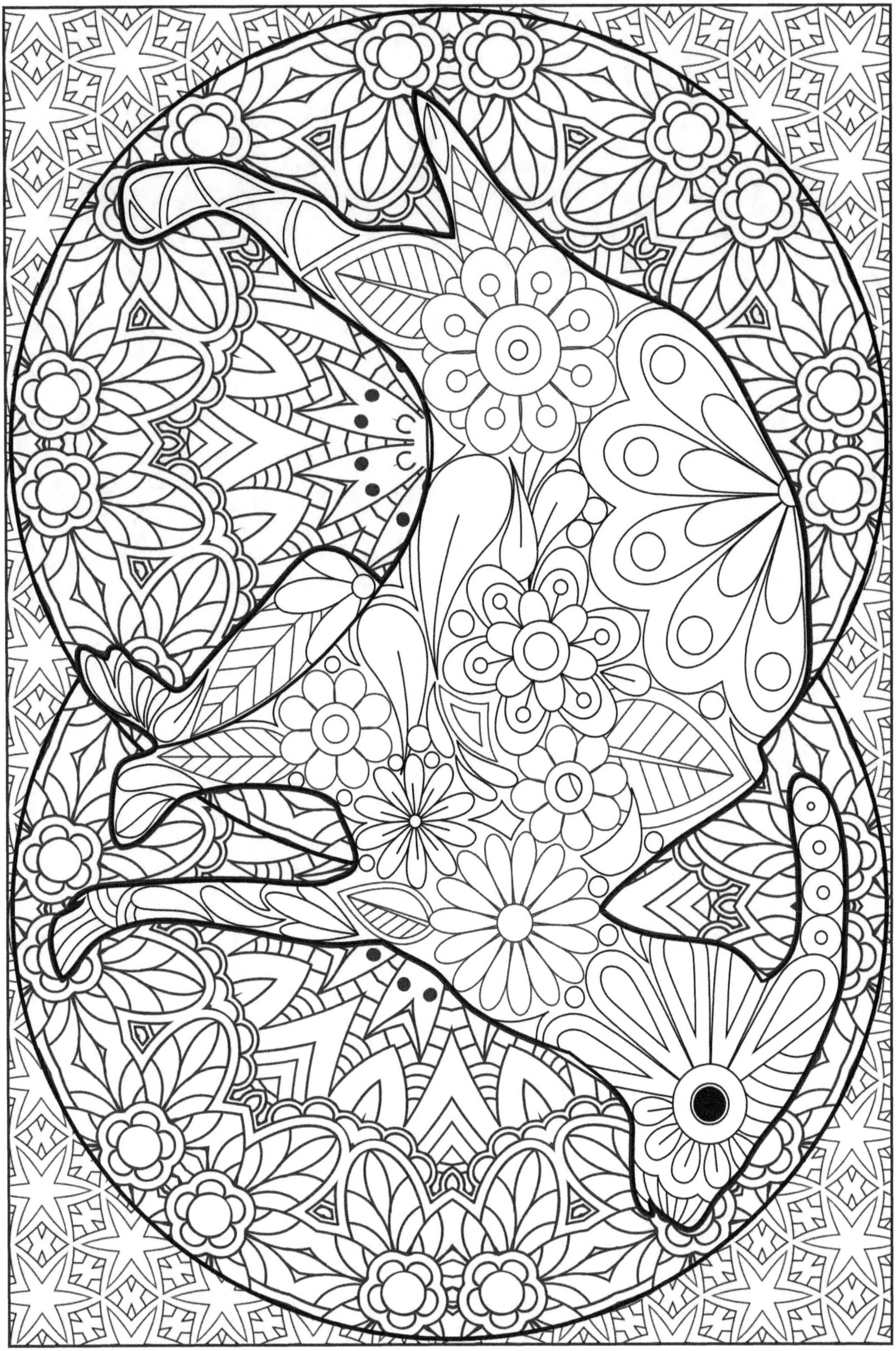

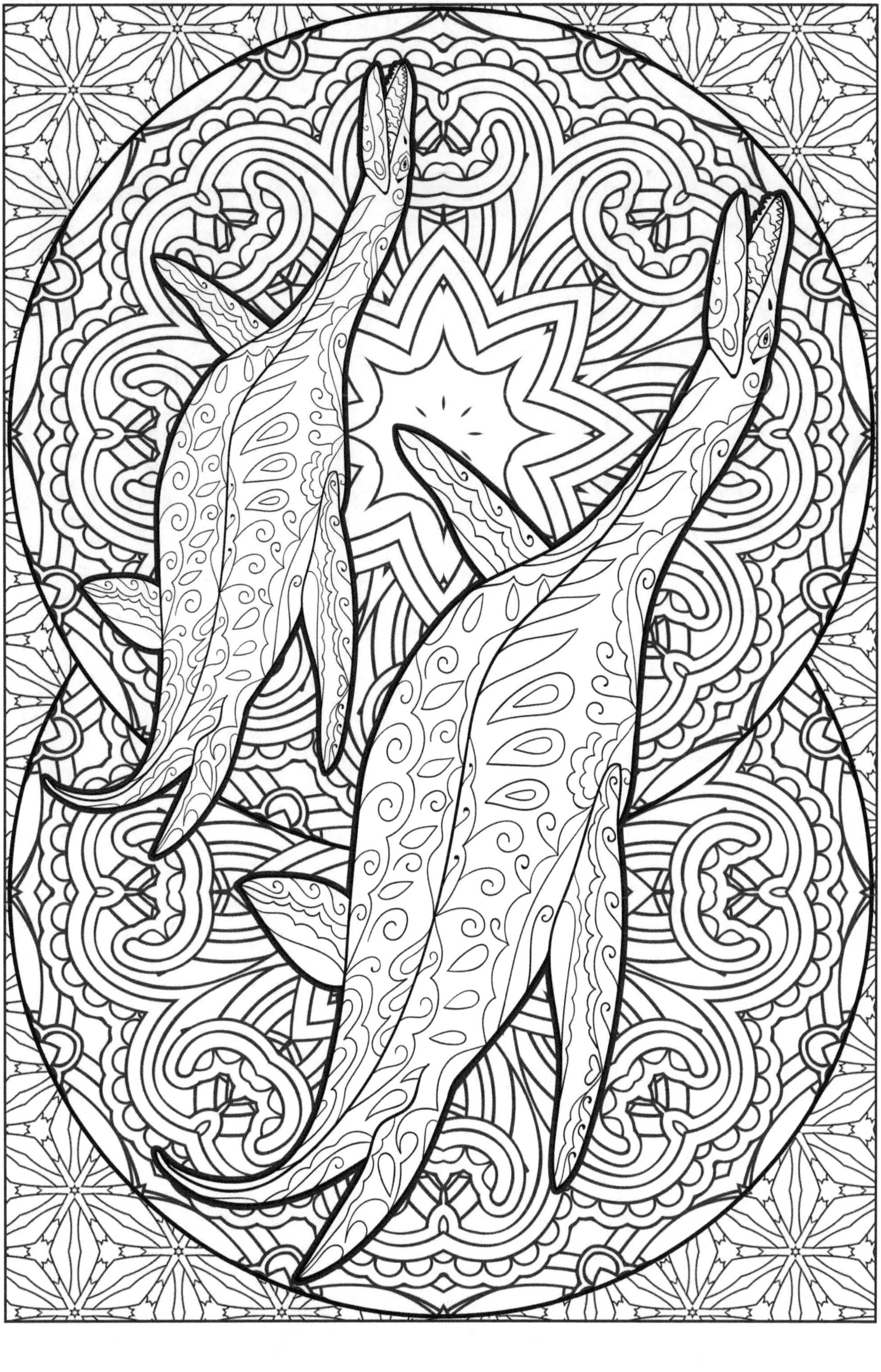

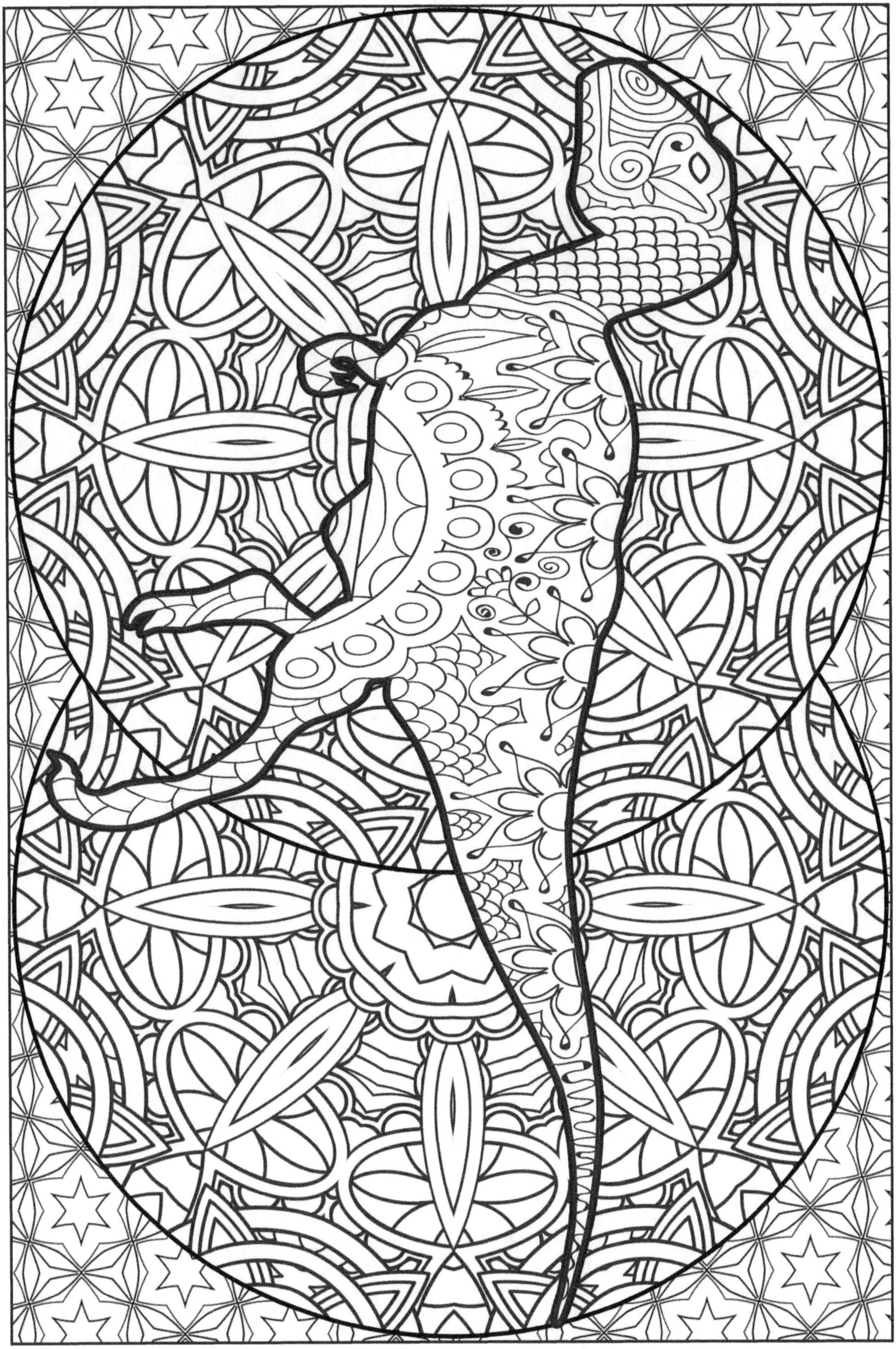

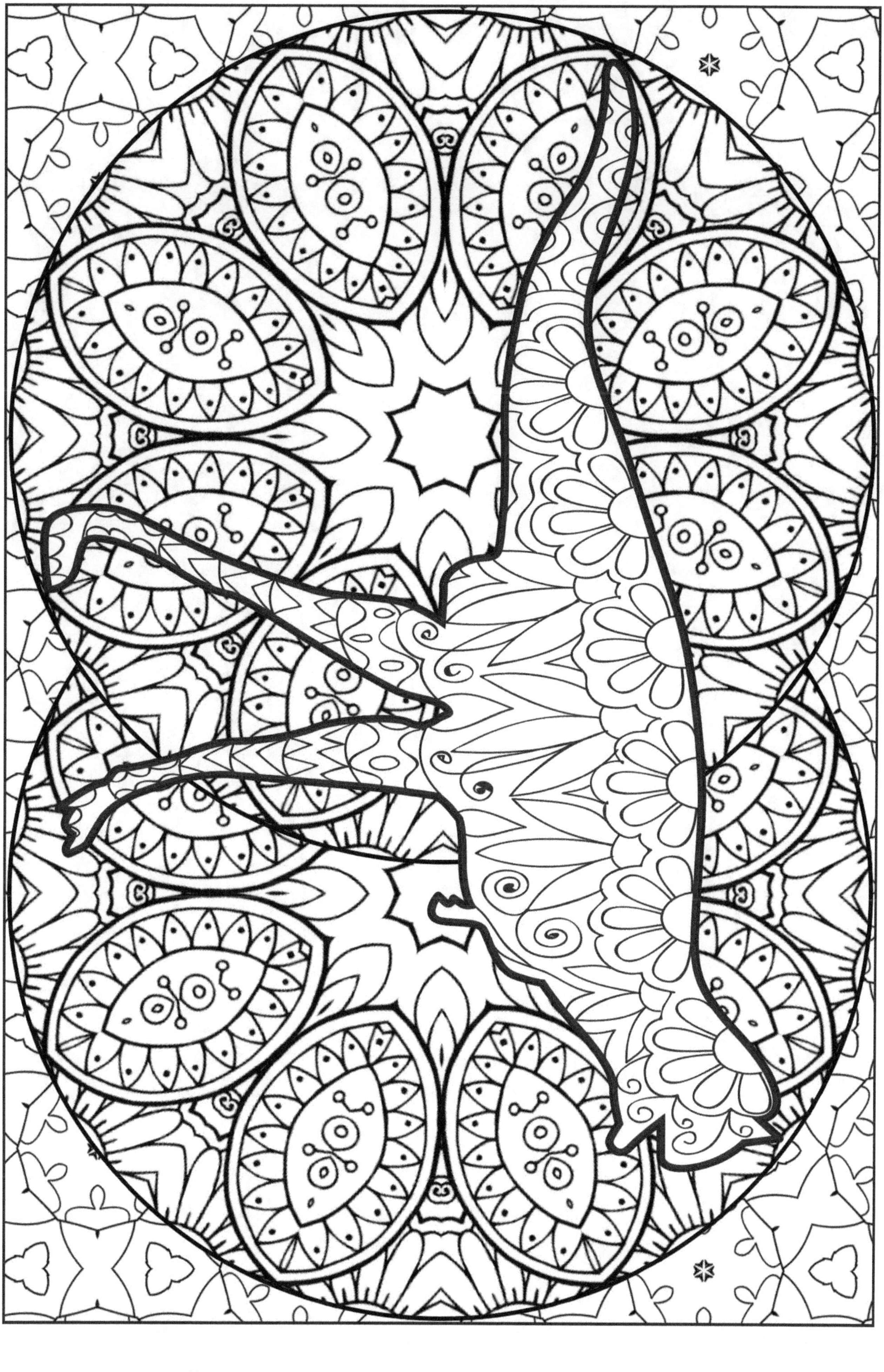

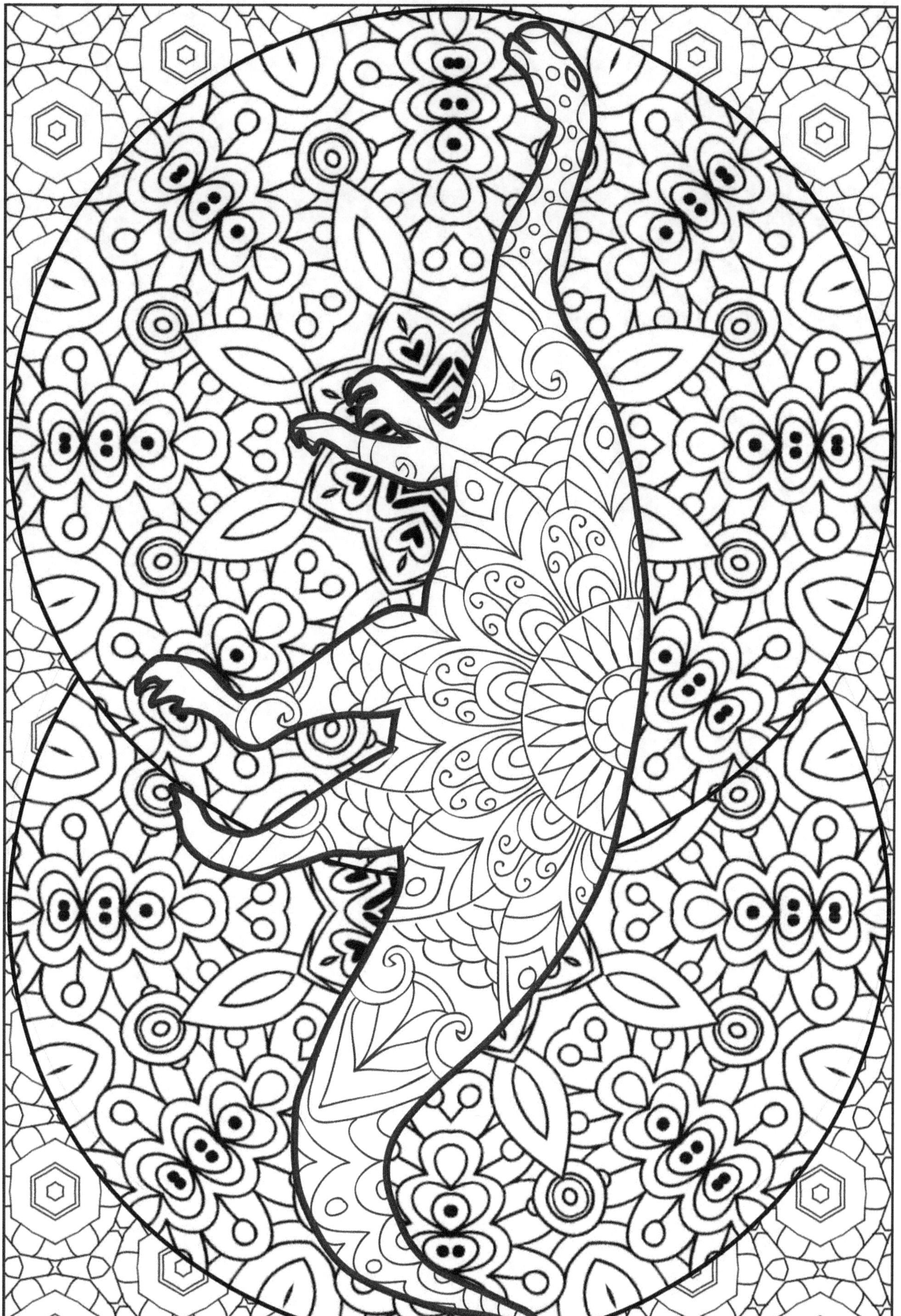

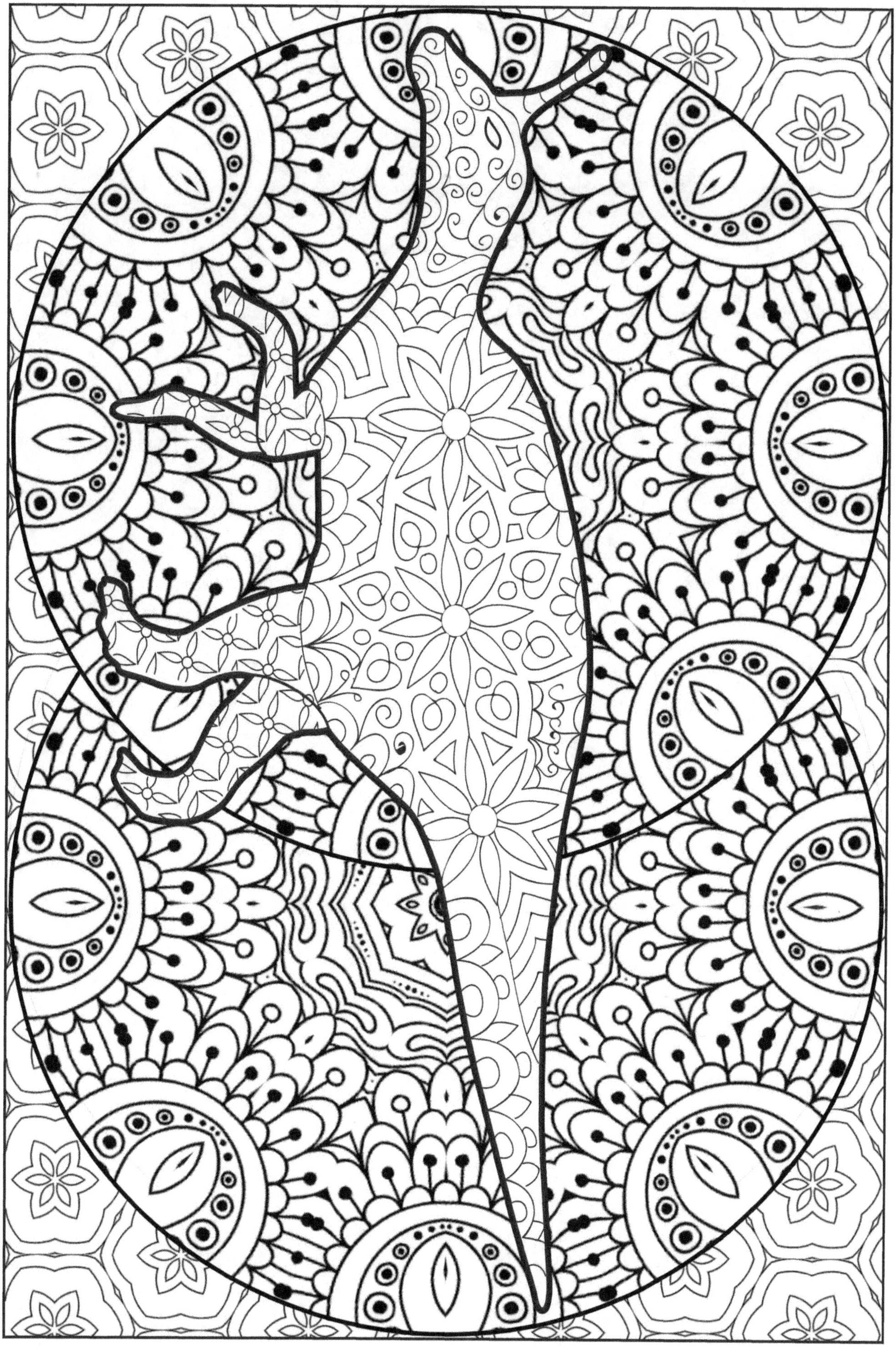

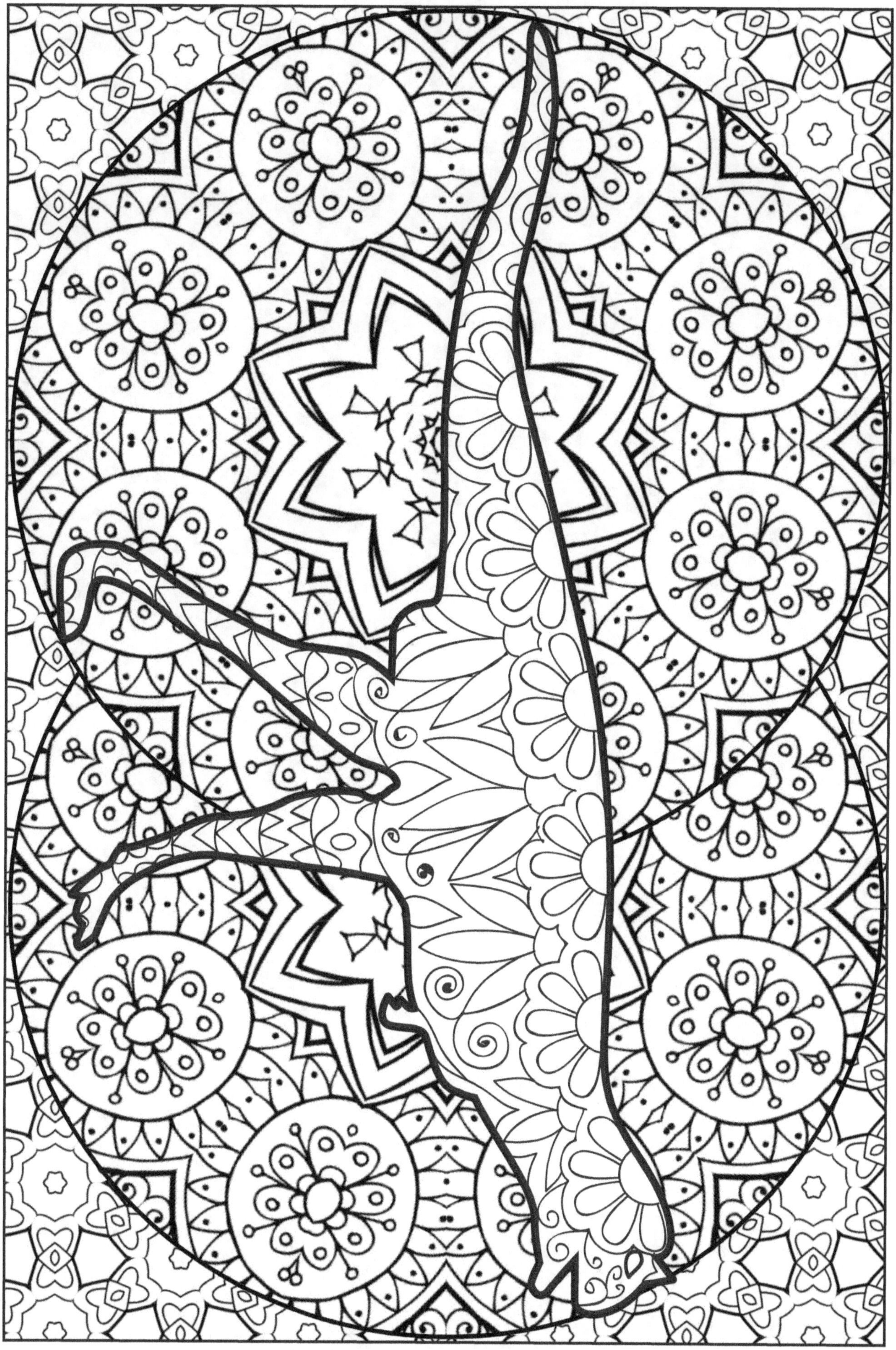

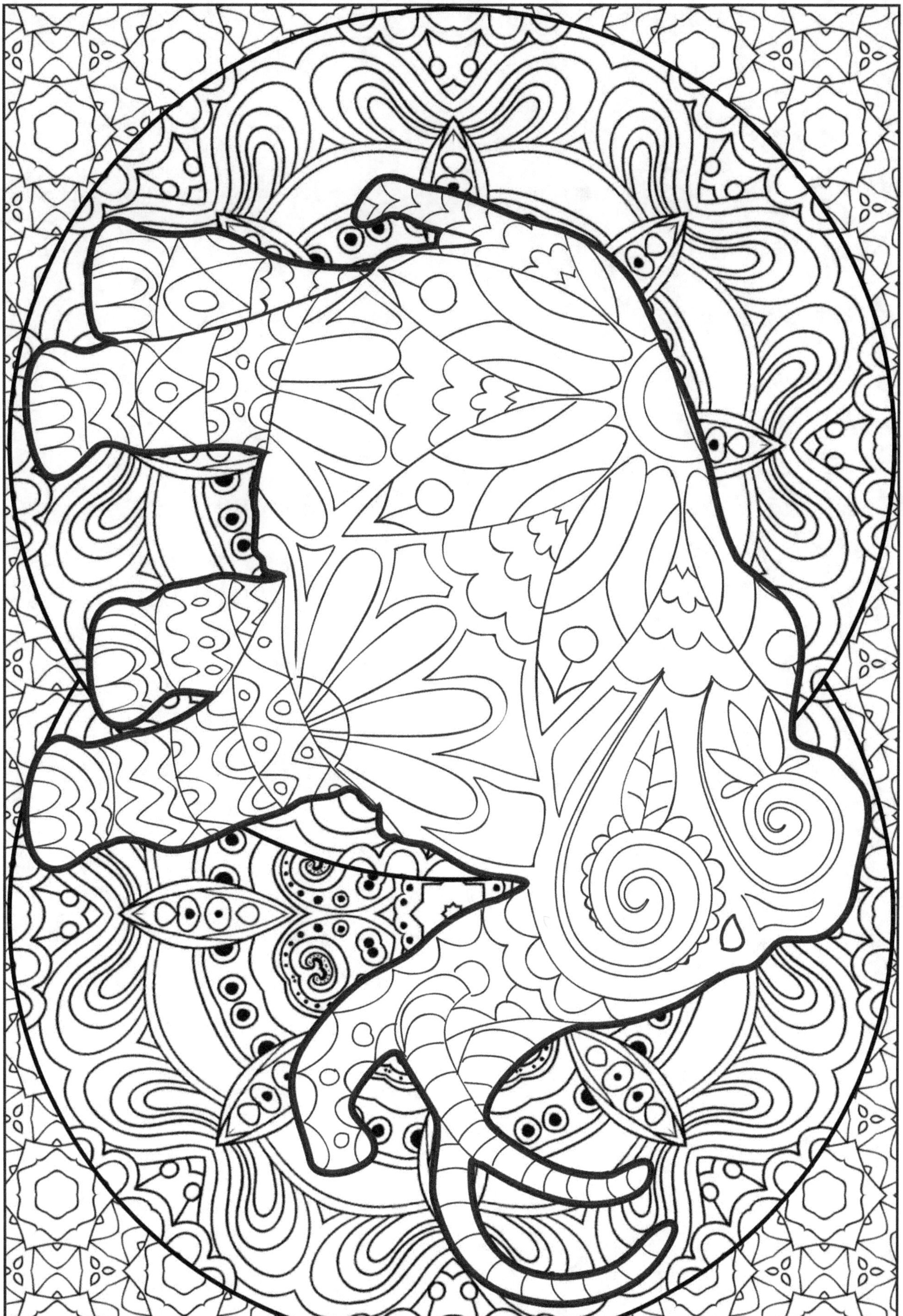

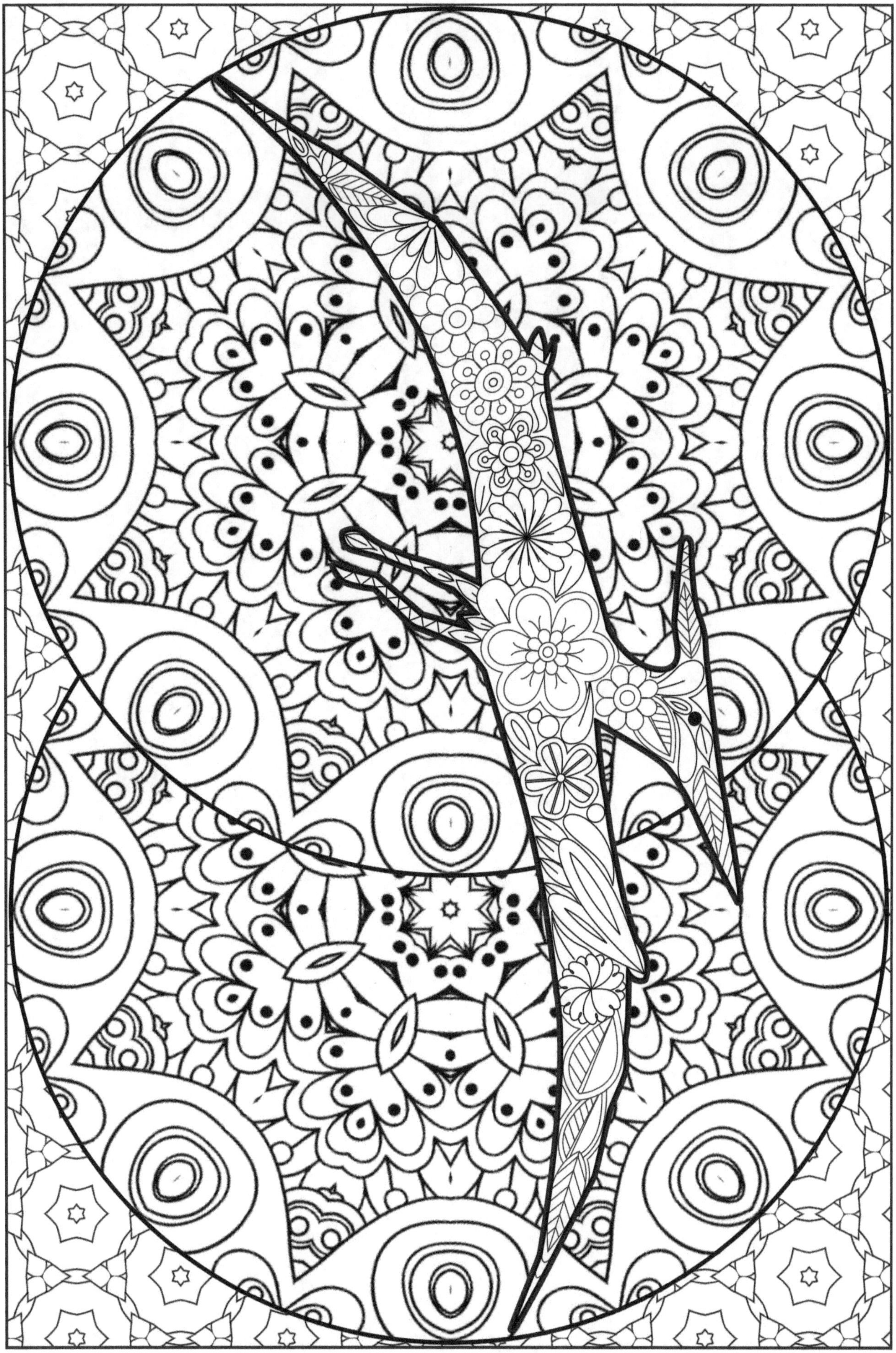

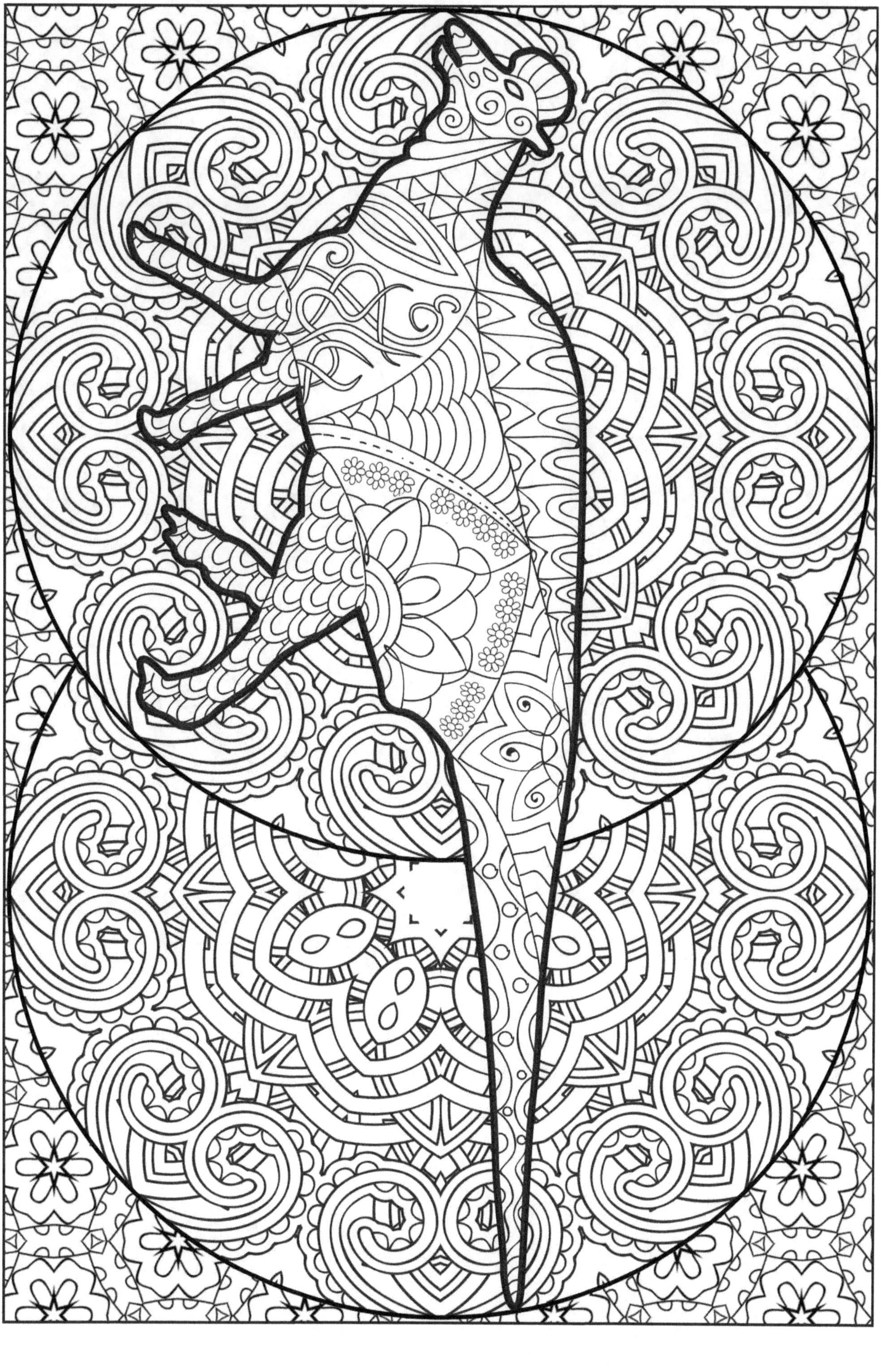

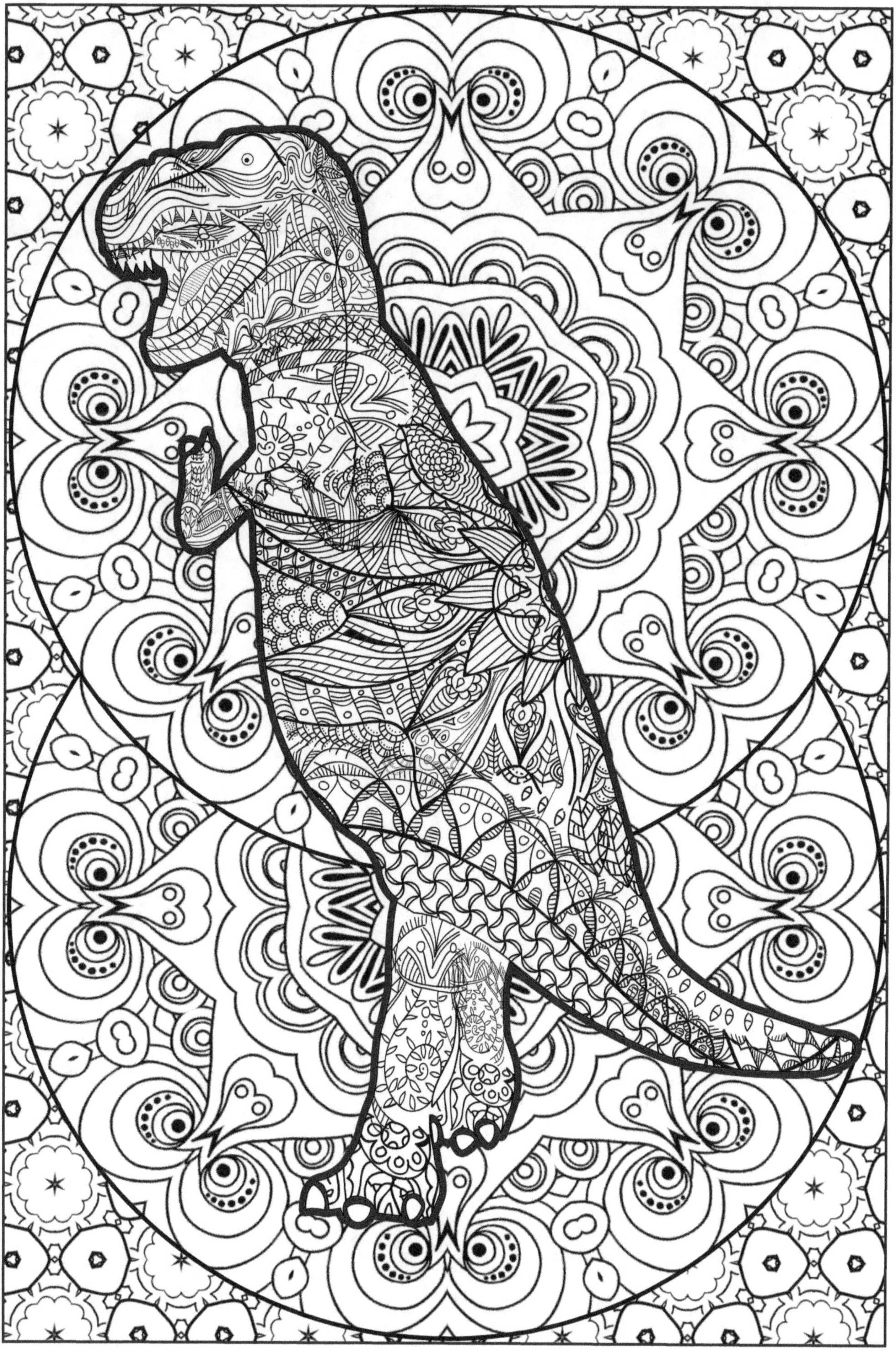

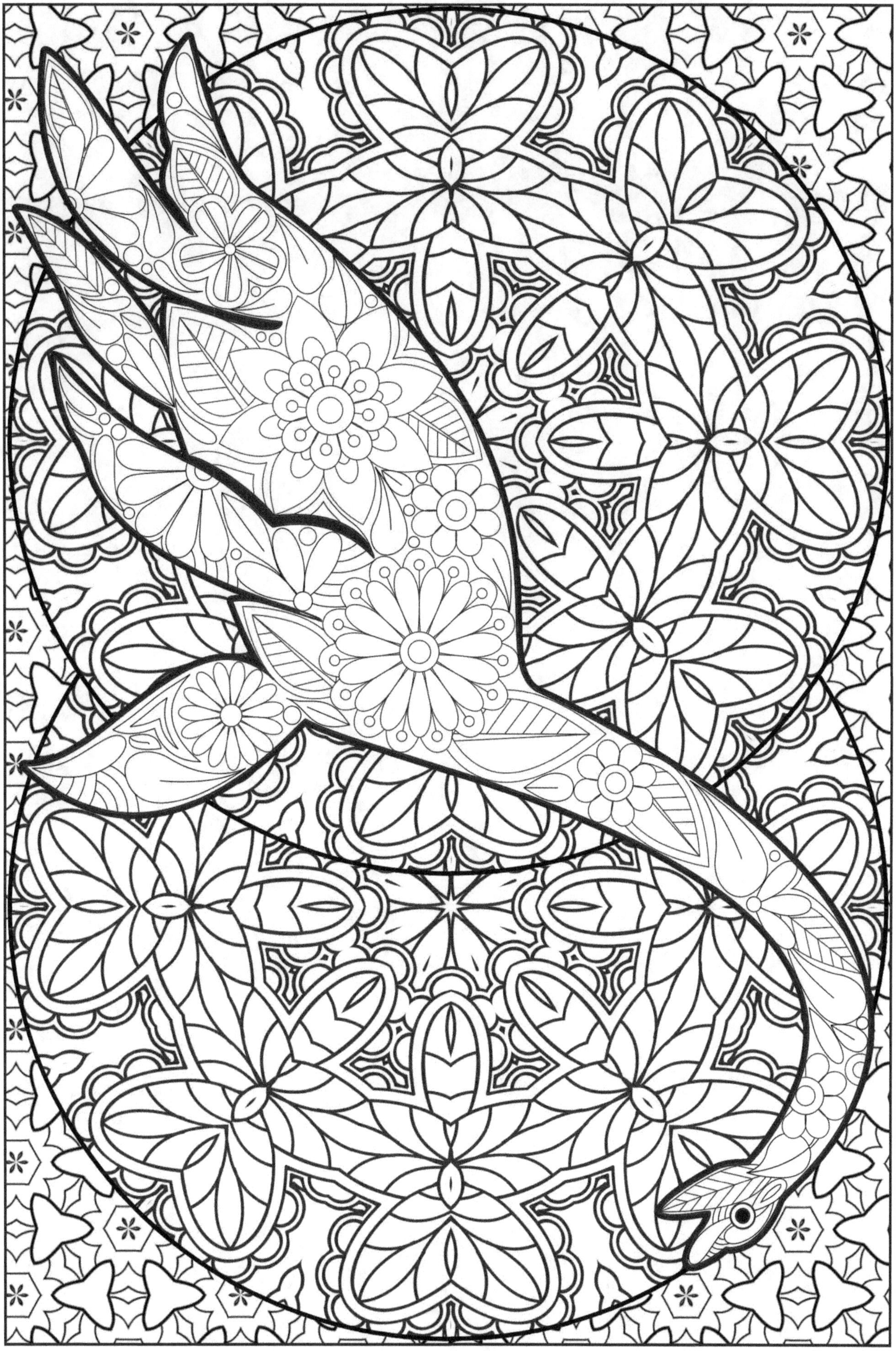

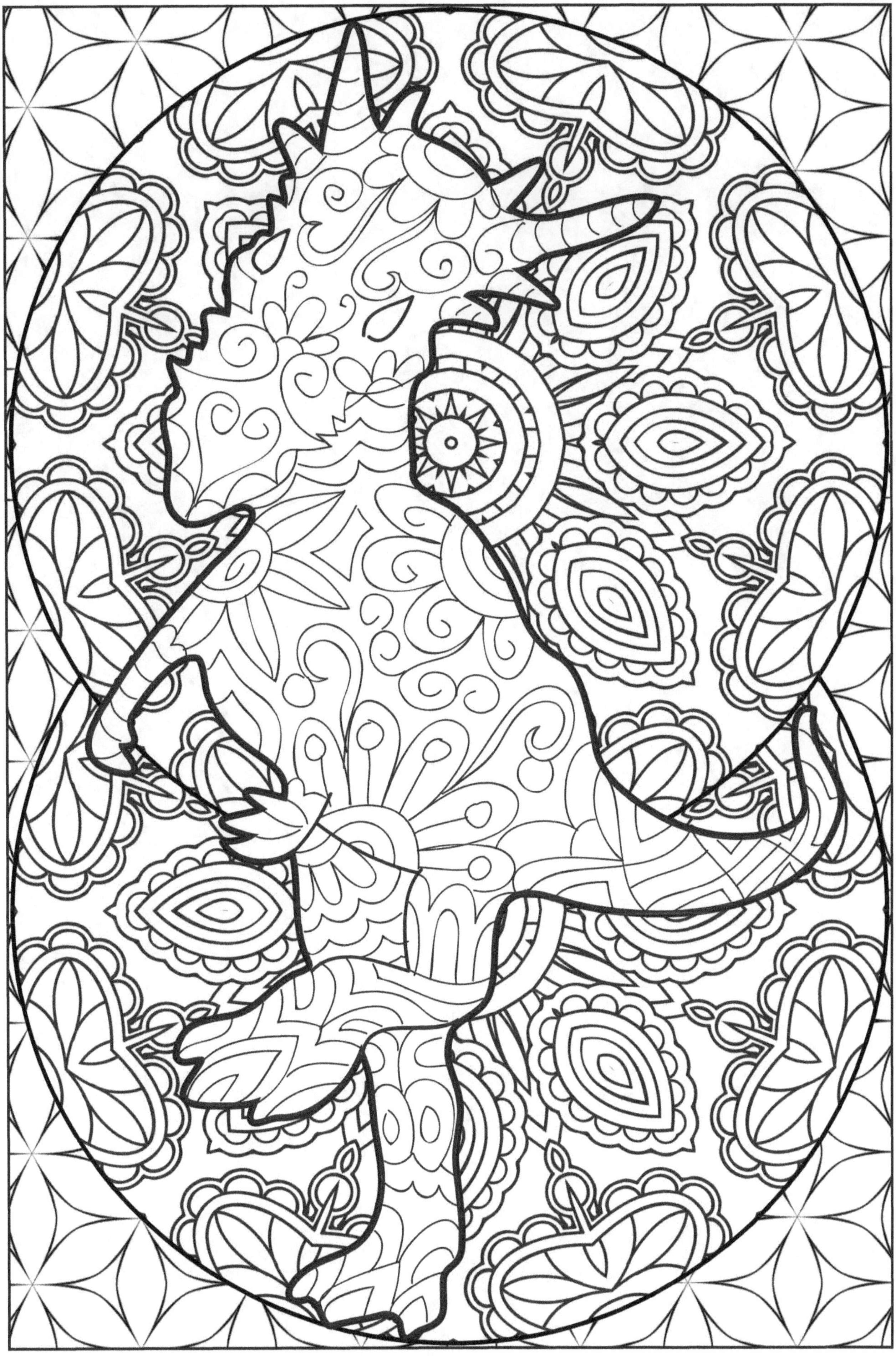

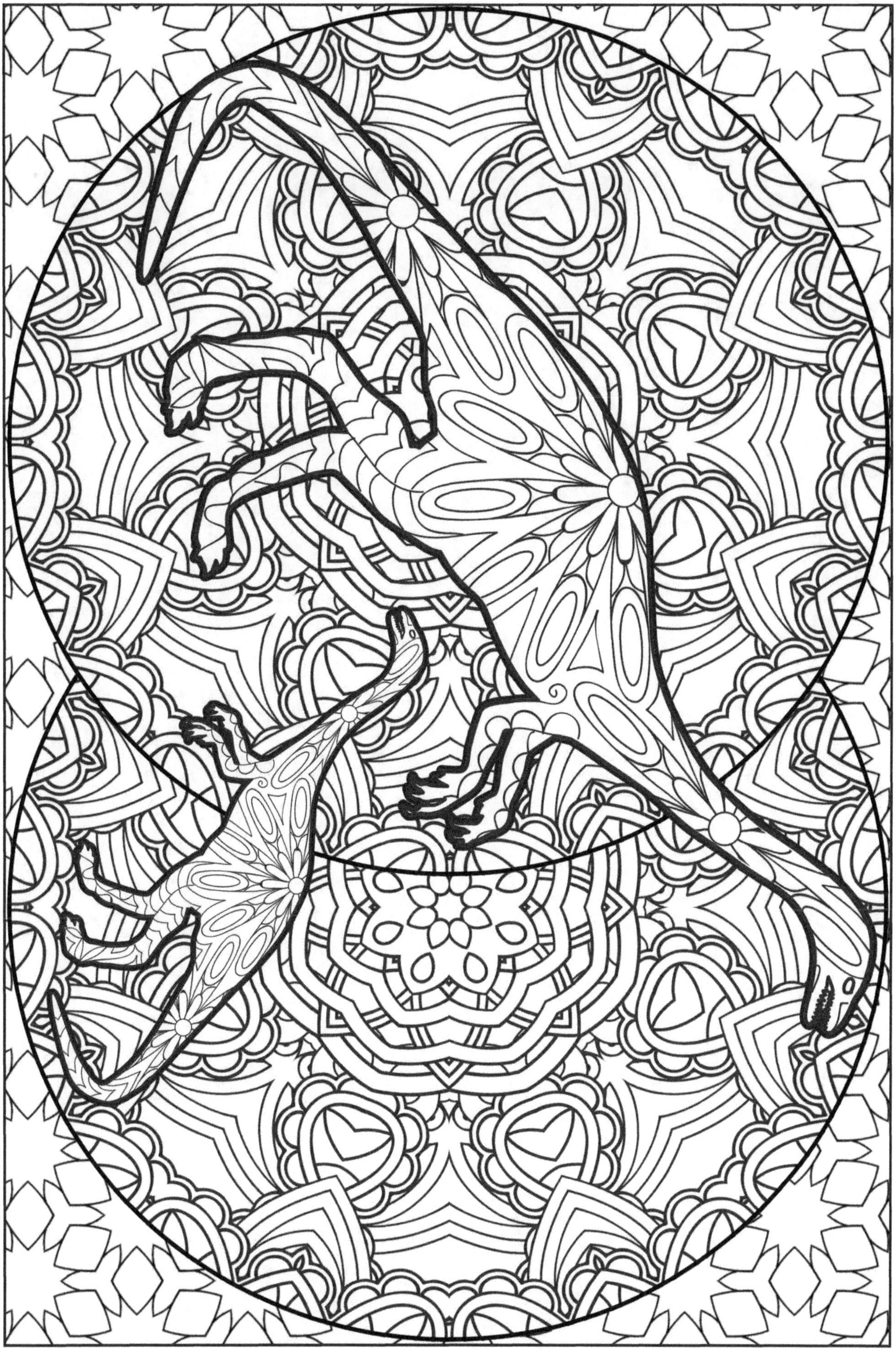

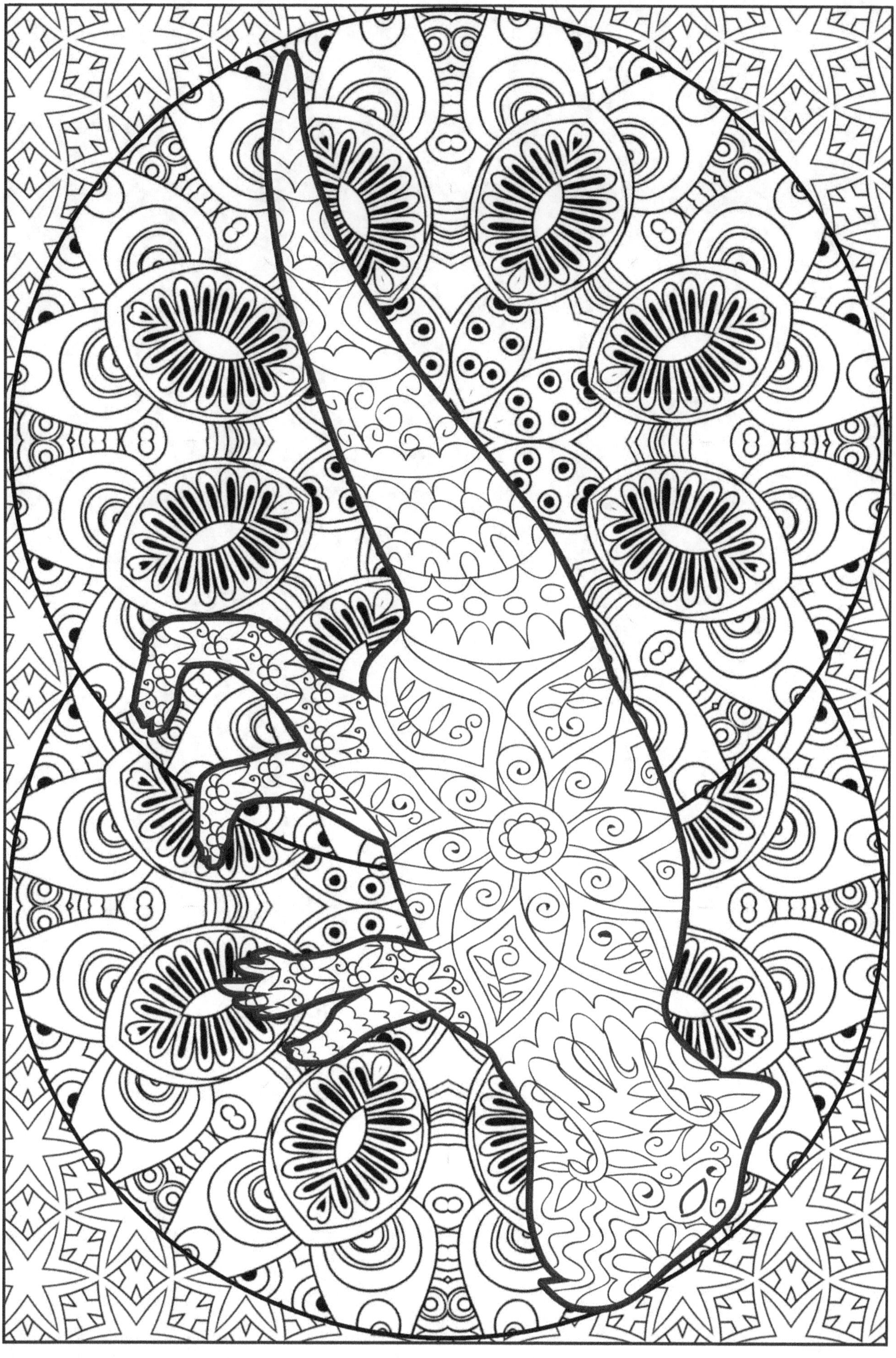

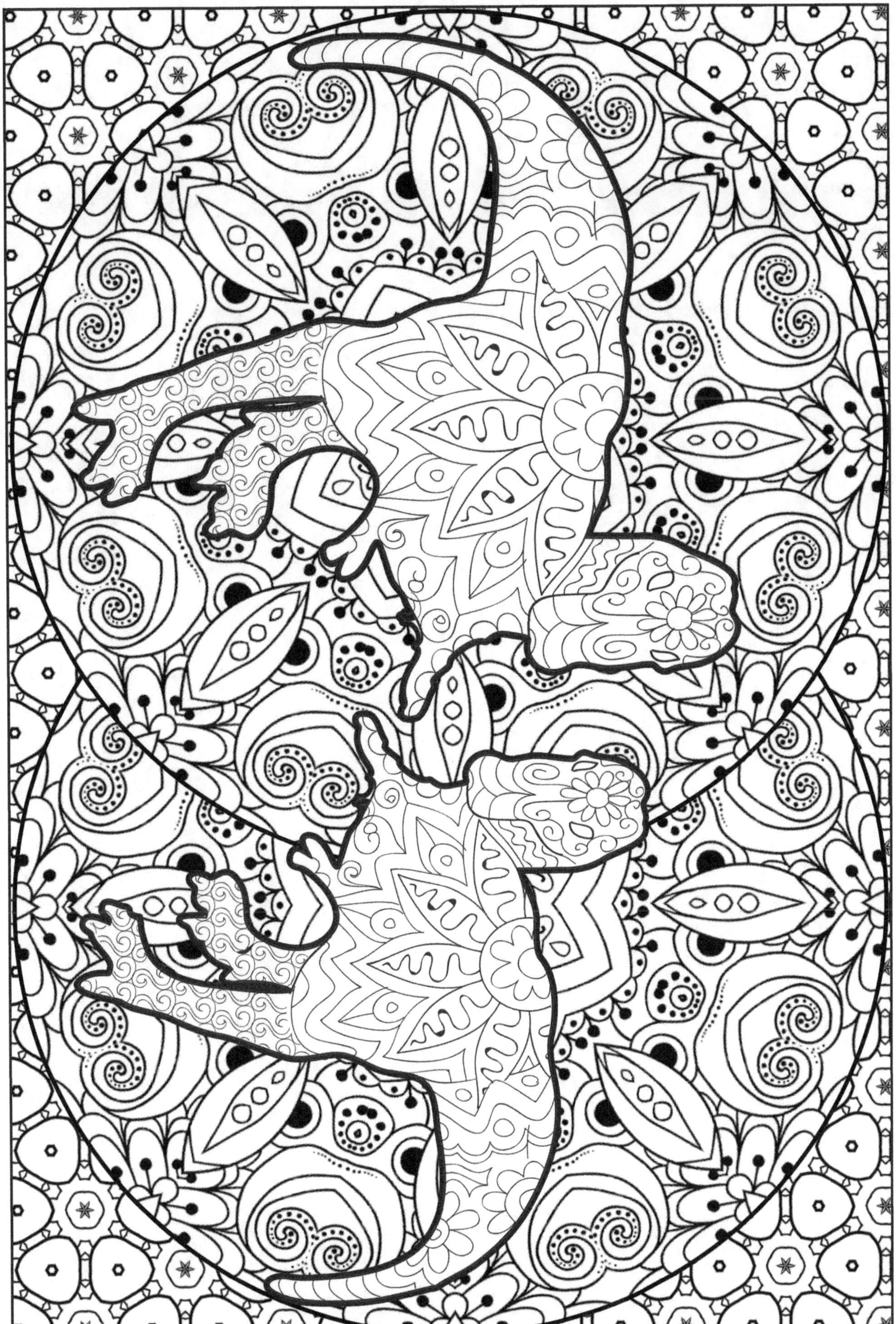

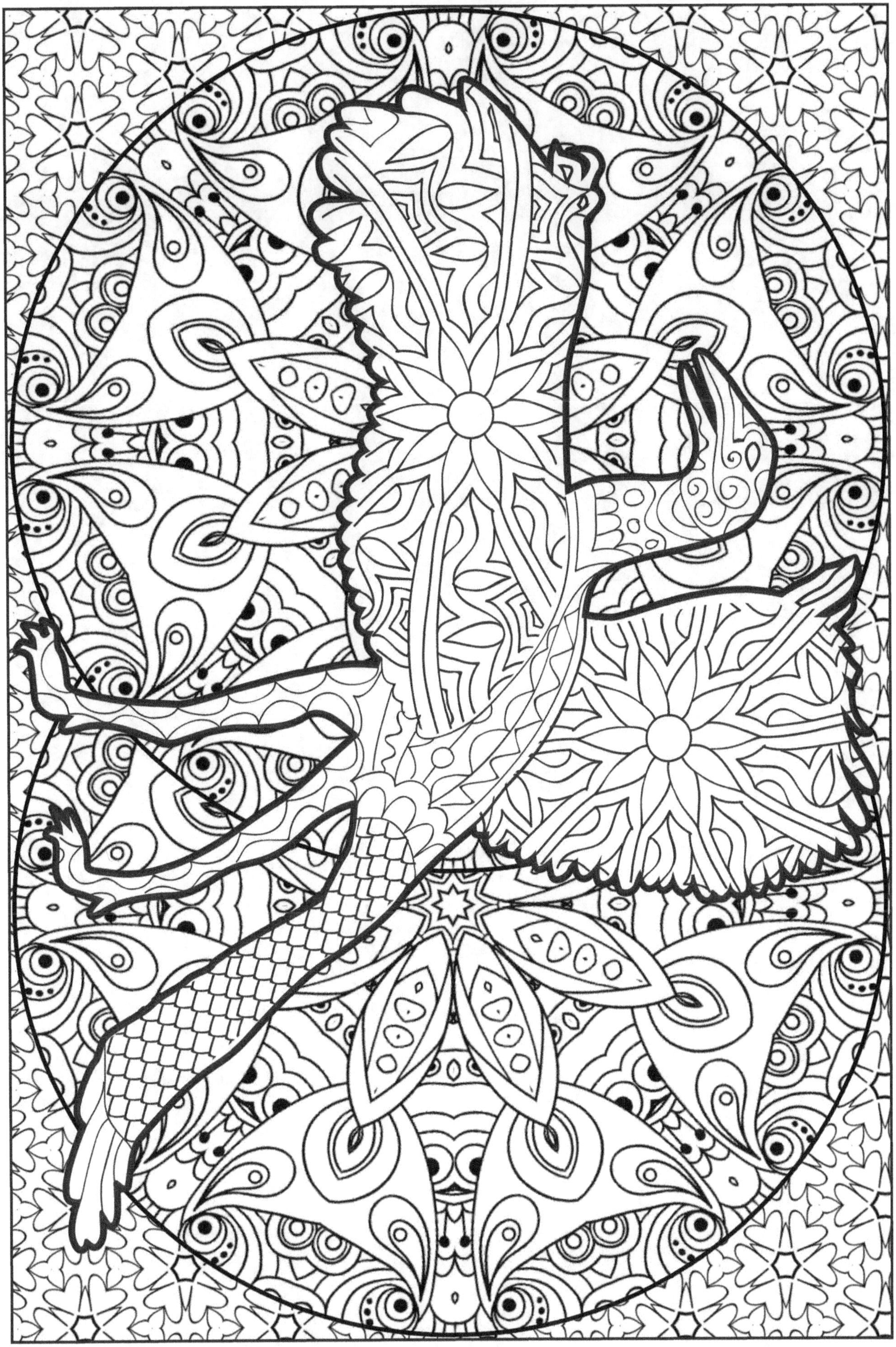

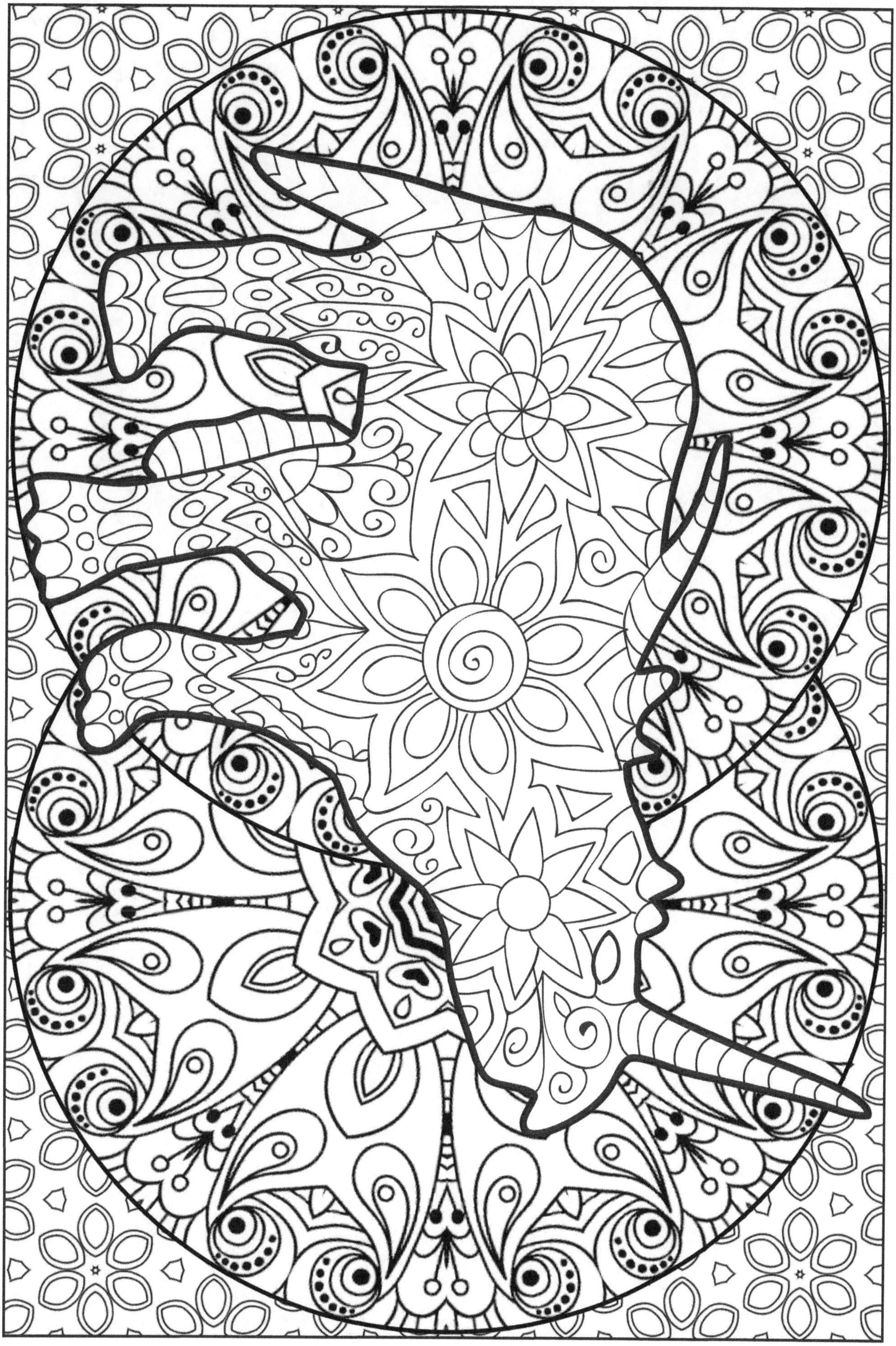

www.ingramcontent.com/pod-product-compliance
Lightning Source LLC
Chambersburg PA
CBHW080540190526
45169CB00007B/2570
9781534850293